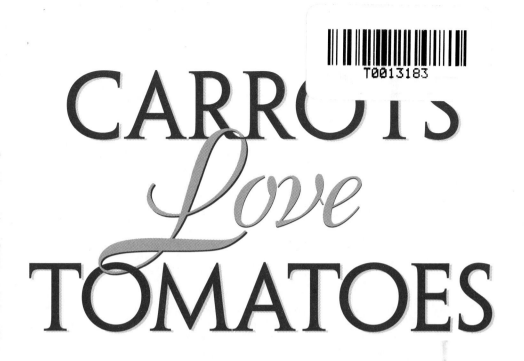

CARROTS
Love
TOMATOES

SECRETS OF COMPANION PLANTING FOR SUCCESSFUL GARDENING

LOUISE RIOTTE

Storey Publishing

The mission of Storey Publishing is to serve our customers by publishing practical information that encourages personal independence in harmony with the environment.

Edited by Julia Needham and Deborah Burns
Cover design by Meredith Maker
Cover illustration by Linda Devito Soltis
Text design by Cynthia McFarland
Text production by Eileen M. Clawson
Line drawings by the author
Indexed by Susan Olason, Indexes & Knowledge Maps

The information in this book is true and complete to the best of our knowledge. All recommendations are made without guarantee on the part of the author or Storey Publishing. The author and publisher disclaim any liability in connection with the use of this information. For additional information please contact Storey Publishing, 210 MASS MoCA Way, North Adams, MA 01247.

Storey books are available at special discounts when purchased in bulk for premiums and sales promotions as well as for fund-raising or educational use. Special editions or book excerpts can also be created to specification. For details, please call 800-827-8673, or send an email to sales@storey.com.

Printed in the United States by Versa Press
50 49 48 47 46 45 44 43 42 41

Library of Congress Cataloging-in-Publication Data

Riotte, Louise.
    Carrots love tomatoes : secrets of companion planting for successful gardening / Louise Riotte. — 2nd ed.
        p. cm.
    "A Storey Publishing book."
    Rev. ed. of : Secrets of companion planting, © 1975.
    Includes bibliographical references (p.) and index.
    ISBN 978-1-58017-027-7 (alk. paper)
    1. Companion planting — Dictionaries. 2. Companion crops — Dictionaries. 3. Gardening — Dictionaries. 4. Plants, Useful — Dictionaries. I. Riotte, Louise. Secrets of companion planting. II. Title.
S603.5.R56 1998
635 — dc21
                                      97-31914
                                         CIP

Table of Contents

Introduction

The magic and mystery of companion
planting have intrigued and fascinated humans
for centuries, yet it is a part of the gardening
world that has never been fully
explored. Even today we are just on
the threshold. In years to come I
hope that scientists, gardeners, and
farmers everywhere will work
together in making more discoveries that will prove of
great value in aug-
menting the world's
food supply.

Plants that
assist each other to grow
well, plants that repel insects, even
plants that repel other plants — all are of
great practical use. They always have been, but we are just beginning to find out why. Delving deeply into this fascinating aspect of
gardening can provide for us both pleasure and very useful information. I hope that what I have written here will give you many of the
tools to work with.

Vegetable growers find that companion planting provides many benefits, one of which is protection from pests. A major enemy of the carrot is the carrot fly, whereas the leek suffers from the onion fly and leek moth. Yet when leek and carrot live together in companionship, the strong and strangely different smell of the partner plant repels the insects so much that they do not even attempt to lay their eggs on the neighbor plant. They take off speedily to get away from the smell. This is why mixed plantings give better insect control than a monoculture, where many plants of the same type are planted together in row after row. Even when plants are affected by diseases, a mixed plant culture can usually alleviate the situation.

It is important to remember that not all "protective" botanicals act quickly. For example, marigolds, to be effective in nematode control, should be grown over at least one full season, and more is better, for their effect is cumulative. One should also realize that certain companion plants will diminish each other's natural repelling ability as they grow together. All through this book you will find "what to grow with" and "what *not* to grow with." Both are equally important to gardening success.

The effects of plants on one another are important outside the vegetable garden, among trees and shrubs as well as grains, grasses, and field crops. These have chapters to themselves, as do herbs, the group of plants most widely used as protective companions.

Wild plants also play a vital part in the plant community. Some are accumulator plants — those that have the ability to collect trace minerals from the soil. They actually can store in their tissues up to several hundred times the amount contained in an equal amount of soil. These plants, many of which are considered weeds, are useful as compost, green manure, or mulch. Some are "deep diggers," sending their roots deep into the ground to penetrate hardpan and helping to condition the soil, and some have value as protectors of garden plants.

• • •

An entirely different type of community life is that of fruit and nut trees and the bush and bramble small fruits. For many of this group, the choice of good companions is not only helpful but also essential. Have you ever experienced the disappointment of having a beautiful fruit tree blossom, be visited by the bees, and yet fail to bear? There is a reason, of course, and it lies in pollinization. Pollen is the dust from blossoms that is needed to make the plant fruitful. If the tree is self-unfruitful and there is no pollenizer of the correct type growing near, it is doubtful that the tree will ever bear well. In the chapters on fruit and nut growing, I'll attempt to unravel some of this mystery, which seems particularly to plague new gardeners and orchardists.

• • •

A note on the chapter devoted to poisonous plants: This information is not meant to frighten but to warn, for most of the nursery catalogs do not tell us which plants are poisonous or to what degree. Even some of the gardening encyclopedias do not.

Cases of death resulting from poisonous plants are rare, but they do happen. In this book I refer to poisonous plants that are useful in the garden for various reasons. It is only fair to tell you that some of those most commonly used may be harmful to children, to livestock, or even to you.

Many of our loveliest and most decorative plants are poisonous — oleanders, daffodils, scillas, lily of the valley, hyacinths, and larkspurs. Other equally poisonous plants are of value for medicines or as insect repellents. To know is to be forewarned, and because we know, we may use them safely, for poisonous plants, unlike poisonous insects or animals, are never aggressive. You are in control of them at all times.

• • •

All of the suggestions given in this book for companion planting are only a beginning. I have included practical information on
soil improvement and garden techniques, as well as some sample
garden plans, to help you put companion
plants to work for you. Your own
experiments will lead you into many
exciting pathways and discoveries.

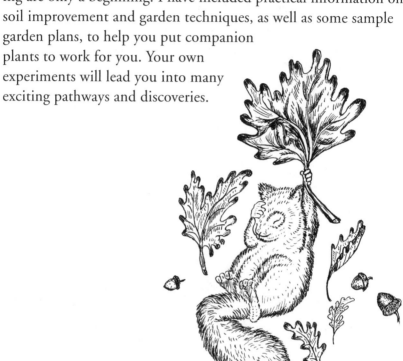

Vegetables

Asparagus *(Asparagus officinalis)*
Parsley planted with asparagus gives added vigor to both.
Asparagus also does well with basil, which itself is a good companion for tomatoes. Tomatoes will protect asparagus against asparagus beetles because they contain a substance called solanine. But if asparagus beetles are present in great numbers, they will attract and be controlled by their natural predators, making spraying unnecessary. A chemical derived from asparagus juice also has been found effective on tomato plants as a killer of nematodes, including root-knot, sting, stubby root, and meadow nematodes.

In my garden I grow asparagus in a long row at one side. After the spears are harvested in early spring I plant tomatoes on either side, and find that both plants prosper from the association. Cultivating the tomatoes also keeps down the weeds from the asparagus. The asparagus fronds should never be cut, if at all, until very late in the fall, as the roots need this top growth to enable them to make spears the following spring.

Bean *(Phaseolus* and *Vicia)*
Many different kinds of beans have been developed, each with its own lore of "good" and "bad" companions. Generally speaking,

however, all will thrive when interplanted with carrots and cauliflower, the carrots especially helping the beans to grow. Beans grow well with beets, too, and are of aid to cucumbers and cabbages.

A moderate quantity of beans planted with leek and celeriac will help all, but planted too thickly they have an inhibiting effect, causing all three to make poor growth. Marigolds in bean rows help repel the Mexican bean beetle.

Summer savory with green beans improves their growth and flavor as well as deterring bean beetles. It is also very good to cook with beans.

Beans are inhibited by any member of the Onion family — garlic, shallots, or chives — and they also dislike being planted near gladiolus.

Broad beans are excellent companions with corn, climbing diligently up the cornstalks to reach the light. They not only anchor the corn more firmly, acting as a protection against the wind, but a heavy vine growth may also act as a deterrent to raccoons. Beans also increase the soil's nitrogen, which is needed by the corn.

Bean, Bush *(Phaseolus vulgaris)*

Included with bush beans are those known as butter, green, snap, string, and wax beans. All will do well when planted with a moderate amount of celery, about one celery plant to every six or seven of beans.

Bush beans do well also when planted with cucumbers. They are mutually beneficial. Bush beans planted in strawberry rows are mutually helpful, both advancing more rapidly than if planted alone.

Bush beans will aid corn if planted in alternate rows. They grow well with summer savory but never should be planted near fennel. They also dislike onions, as do all beans.

Bean, Lima *(Phaseolus limensis)*

Nearby locust trees have a good effect on the growth of lima beans. Other plants give them little or no assistance in repelling insects. Never cultivate lima beans when they are wet, because if anthracnose is present, this will cause it to spread. If the ground has sufficient lime and phosphorus, there will probably be little trouble from anthracnose and mildew.

Bean, Pole
Like others of the family, pole beans do well with corn and summer savory. They also have some pronounced dislikes, such as kohlrabi and sunflower. Beets do not grow well with them but radishes and pole beans seem to derive mutual benefit.

Beet *(Beta vulgaris)*
Beets grow well near bush beans, onions, and kohlrabi but are "turned off" by pole beans. Field mustard and charlock inhibit their growth. Lettuce and most members of the Cabbage family are "friendly" to them.

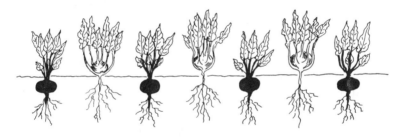

Beets and kohlrabi make good companions. Both take the same kind of culture, and they take soil nourishment at different levels.

Broccoli *(Brassica oleraceae)*
Like all members of the Cabbage family, broccoli does well with such aromatic plants as dill, celery, camomile, sage, peppermint, and rosemary, and with other vegetables such as potatoes, beets, and onions. Do not plant it with tomatoes, pole beans, or strawberries. Use pyrethrum on broccoli against aphids, before the flower buds open. (See the Pest Control chapter.)

If rabbits dig your cabbage patch, plant any member of the onion family among them. Or you can dust with ashes, powdered aloes, or cayenne pepper. Rabbits also shun dried blood and blood meal.

Cabbage (Brassicaceae)

The cabbage family includes not only cabbage but cauliflower, kale, kohlrabi, broccoli, collards, and Brussels sprouts — even rutabaga and turnip. While each plant of this group has been developed in a special way, they are all pretty much subject to the same likes and dislikes, insects and diseases. Hyssop, thyme, wormwood, and southernwood are helpful in repelling the white cabbage butterfly.

All members of the family are greatly helped by aromatic plants or those that have many blossoms. Good companions are celery, dill, camomile, sage, peppermint, rosemary, onions, and potatoes. Cabbages dislike strawberries, tomatoes, and pole beans.

All members of the family are heavy feeders and should have plenty of compost or well-decomposed cow manure worked into the ground previous to planting. Mulching will help if soil has a tendency to dry out in hot weather, and water should be given if necessary.

Butterflies themselves do no harm and can help pollinate plants. It is their caterpillars that do much damage to the orchard and field crops. The white cabbage butterfly is perhaps the most destructive. Herbs will repel them: hyssop, peppermint, rosemary, sage, thyme, and southernwood.

Cabbage and cauliflower are subject to clubroot, and if this occurs, try new soil in a different part of the garden. Dig to a depth of 12 inches and incorporate plenty of well-rotted manure into the soil. Rotate cabbage crops every two years.

If cabbage or broccoli plants do not head up well, it is a sign that lime, phosphorus, or potash is needed. Boron deficiency may cause the heart of cabbage to die out.

Carrot *(Daucus carota)*

For sweet-tasting carrots your soil must have sufficient lime, humus, and potash. Too much nitrogen will cause poor flavor, as will a long period of hot weather.

Onions, leeks, and herbs such as rosemary, wormwood, and sage act as repellents to the carrot fly *(Psila rosae),* whose maggot or

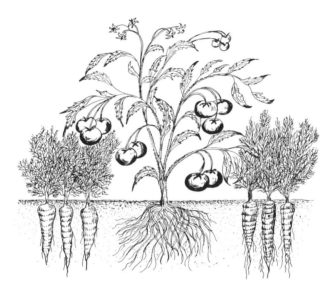

Carrots are good to grow with tomatoes — also with leaf lettuce, chives, onions, leeks, radishes, rosemary, and sage. They have a pronounced dislike for dill. Carrot roots themselves contain an exudate beneficial to the growth of peas.

larva often attacks the rootlets of young plants. Black salsify *(Scorzonera hispanica),* sometimes called oyster plant, also is effective in repelling the carrot fly. Use as a mixed crop.

Apples and carrots should be stored a distance from each other to prevent the carrots from taking on a bitter flavor.

Cauliflower (Brassicaceae)
The white cabbage butterfly *(Pieris rapae)* is repelled if celery plants are grown near the cauliflower, but cauliflower does not like tomatoes or strawberries. Extract from cauliflower seeds inactivates the bacteria causing black rot.

Celeriac *(Apium graveolens rapaceum)*
A sowing of winter vetch before planting celeriac is helpful, for the plant needs a rich, loose soil with plenty of potassium. The leek, also a potassium lover, is a good companion in alternating rows, as are scarlet runner beans.

Celeriac does not need as much attention as celery since blanching is not necessary, but as the root starts to enlarge, the crown may be helped to better development and higher quality by removing the fine roots and the soil attached to them. Many lateral roots close to the top of the crown tend to make the fleshy part irregular and coarse.

Celery *(Apium graveolens)*

Celery grows well with leeks, tomatoes, cauliflower, and cabbage, while bush beans and celery seem to give mutual assistance. One gardener believes that celery is particularly benefited if grown in a circle so that the lacy, loosely interwoven roots may make a more desirable home for earthworms and soil microbes. Celery and leeks both grow well when trenched.

Both celery and celeriac are reported to have a hormone that has an effect similar to insulin, making them an excellent seasoning for diabetics or for anyone on a salt-reduced diet.

Celery dinant or French celery dinant is a unique type that sends out a multitude of narrow stalks. I have found it easy to grow here in southern Oklahoma. It has a much fuller flavor than common celery and less should be used in cooking.

This celery is completely insect-free and grows well with all garden vegetables. Plants will freeze in winter but the root does not, and will put out new leaves from the center with the advent of warm spring weather. In a cold climate the leaves may be dried for winter use.

Chayote *(Sechium edule)*

This is a perennial tropical vine, an annual in colder climates, which bears a delicious, light green, pear-shaped fruit in the fall. Two vines must be grown or it will not bear well. Chayotes in a cream sauce are a dish "fit for the gods." I grow them on my garden fence along with cucumbers, where both do exceptionally well. They apparently have no insect enemies and seem to be protective to the cucumbers.

Chile Peppers (*Capsicum* spp.)

The Aztec "chilli" or the Spanish "chile" is known to have existed as early as 700 B.C., but its birthplace remains a mystery, says Anne Lindsay Greer writing in *Cuisine of the American Southwest*. She also claims that all chiles contain an element of unpredictability but insists that all Mexican food or all chiles are not hot. More chiles are produced and consumed than any other seasoning in the world. The hotness of each depends on the climate in which it is grown.

Early South and Central American cultures used chiles for medicinal purposes, currency, and as a discipline for disobedient children. Chiles are thought to be an aid to digestion, to give protection from colds, and to cure everything from toothache to colic to an indifference toward romance. But after separating fact from folklore, some of the mystique from chiles, certain facts remain undisputed:

- Chiles are high in vitamins A and C. One ounce of dried chile has two times the daily requirement of vitamin A.
- Chiles serve as a natural meat preservative by retarding the oxidation of fats.
- Chiles added personality and flavor to the otherwise bland diet of early southwesterners.
- Chiles can be used to reduce the amount of salt in many dishes, or eliminate salt altogether for those on a low-sodium diet.

Columbus is said to have discovered chiles in the West Indies (though he called them peppers). Thereafter they were enthusiastically adopted by the rest of the world. Indian food, Szechuan sauces, Cajun cooking, and southern African cuisines all favor chiles for their assertive flavors. Southwestern and Asian recipes are becoming increasingly popular and many call for chile peppers.

Chiles can be direct seeded after the last spring frost in long, warm-season areas or sown indoors 6 to 8 weeks before transplanting out. Chile peppers are easily transplanted, and most produce fruits with almost reckless abandon!

A CHILE LINEUP

'Habanero'. Hottest! Lantern-shaped, lime green to orange fruit. Aromatic and tasty in sauces or pickled. Wear gloves when preparing this chile.

'Piquin'. Very hot, round, or slightly pointed, perennial in Mexico and south Texas.

'Thai Pepper'. Tiny peppers (1 inch long), red when ripe, bred in Thailand, hot and the heat lingers. Use in Oriental dishes.

'Anaheim "M" Chili'. An 8-inch long, tapering chile, which can be used green for rellenos and green chile sauce, or dry in red enchilada sauce. A medium-hot, long-bearing pepper.

'Aji'. Hot, fruity Peruvian, a thin orange to red 3–5 inches long.

'Centennial'. Tiny ornamental purple to white to red simultaneously. Hot pods are edible at all stages. (Named for our flag's colors.)

'De Arbol'. Treelike plant; 3–4 feet tall; thin 3–4-inch chiles; hot and smoky. Good for drying.

'Serrano'. Hot, small, slender, rounded chile. Serve fresh, dry, or pickled. Good in salsas. May be frozen if blanched first.

'Cayenne'. Hot, short, slender. Best dried and ground for red-hot sauces. Used in Asian as well as Mexican and southwestern food.

'Sandia Hot'. Very hot, thin-walled, best dried and ground. A standard for hot chile lovers. May be used green or red, fresh or dried.

'Chimayo'. Pick green for your favorite stew or salsa. Dried and ground for red chile powder, it makes an excellent enchilada sauce.

'Española' Improved. A special short-season chile that will turn red and get hot even in northern climates. Narrow, pointed, and thin-walled. Use green or red.

'Jalapeño'. Everybody's favorite. Easily grown, prolific producer. A 3-inch, dark green, almost black chile with thick, meaty walls. Good for pickling or fresh. Finely chopped, adds a new dimension to corn bread.

'Santa Fe Grande'. Short, thick, hot, yellow pepper, good in condiments or pickled. Very attractive as an ornamental.

'Cascabel'. Medium hot, tough, round, and dark red, the 1-inch pod makes a dark, smoky chile pepper.

'NuMex Eclipse'. Dark brown when ripe, medium hot. Adds color to vegetable dishes.

'NuMex Sunrise'. Bright yellow when ripe, medium hot. May be used as a green chile.

'Big Jim'. Five 'Big Jims' may weigh as much as one pound. This pepper is a perfect candidate for chile rellenos.

'Vallero'. Dark red, medium hot. Use dried for red chile sauces and soups.

'Mulatto'. Dark brown when dried, excellent for rellenos, very smoky flavor. 5 inches long, 2-inch pods are mild.

'Guajillo'. Used dry in soups and salsas.

'Andho' ('Poblano'). Large, heart-shaped, mild chile of excellent flavor. Use peeled 'Poblano' for rellenos, or cut into strips for soups and stews. Good dried.

'Pasilla'. Almost black when dried, use for mole. Pods are mild.

'Pimento'. Hungarians use for paprika. Heart-shaped, 4 inches long, red, mild, good stuffed or as a stuffing. Mild to hot.

Chinese Celery Cabbage (Brassica chinensis)

This easy-to-grow vegetable, deserving to be better known in America, is one of the oldest vegetable crops in China. I grow both types: the tall, slender heads and the huge, deeply savoyed hybrid type, which makes a round head. I find that celery cabbage grows well, making enormous heads, if planted in my fall garden about two feet apart. I alternate the plants in the row with Brussels sprouts or cauliflower.

Chinese celery cabbage does well in the fall garden, interplanted with Brussels sprouts.

Celery cabbage has few insect enemies but should not be grown near corn, as the corn worms will infest it.

Collard *(Brassica oleracea,* var. *acephala)*

Cornell University's College of Agriculture has shown that collards benefit from interplanting with tomatoes since the flea beetle, the prime pests of collards, is significantly decreased.

Collards, widely grown in the southern states as a source of greens, are more nutritious than heading cabbage, and their taste is improved by freezing.

Corn *(Zea mays)*

Sweet corn does well with potatoes, peas, beans, cucumbers, pumpkin, and squash. Peas and beans help corn by restoring to the soil the nitrogen used up by the corn. Is there anyone who hasn't heard the story of Indians putting a fish in every corn hill?

Melons, squash, pumpkins, and cucumbers like the shade provided by corn. In turn they benefit the corn, protecting it from the depredations of raccoons, which do not like to travel through the thick vines. Similarly, pole beans may be planted with corn to climb on the stalks. But don't plant tomatoes near corn because the tomato fruitworm and corn earworm are identical.

An experiment with odorless marigold showed that when it was planted next to corn, the Japanese beetle did not chew off the corn silks.

An experiment reported in the British *New Scientist* in 1970 states that, "Reduced incidence of fall armyworm on maize [corn] and a correspondingly increased yield were obtained by growing the crop with sunflower in alternating strips . . . there were also large reductions in the numbers of *Carpophilus* beetles in the sunflower strips, compared with unbroken areas of the crop. Some infestations were cut by more than half."

Research has shown that to remove corn suckers is a waste of time as well as being detrimental to the development of the ears.

Cucumber *(Cucumis sativus)*

Cucumbers apparently are offensive to raccoons, so they are a good plant with corn. And corn seemingly protects the cucumber against the virus that causes wilt. Thin strips of cucumber will repel ants.

Cucumbers also like beans, peas, radishes, and sunflower, and, preferring some shade, they will grow well in young orchards.

Sow two or three radish seeds in cucumber hills to protect against cucumber beetles. Do not pull the radishes, but let them grow as long as they will, even blossoming and going to seed. Cucumber beetles also may be trapped by filling shallow containers about three-fourths full of water into which some cooking oil has been poured.

If cucumbers are attacked by nematodes, try a sugar spray. I boil a half cup of sugar in two cups of water, stirring until completely dissolved. Let cool and dilute with one gallon of water. Strange as it seems, sugar kills nematodes by drying them out. This will also attract honeybees, ensuring pollination and resulting in a bumper crop of cucumbers, so the spray is worth trying even if you don't suspect the presence of nematodes.

Beneficial fungi are another enemy of nematodes. If you suspect their presence, build up the humus content of your soil.

A chive spray is helpful for downy mildew on cucumbers, as is a spray made of horsetail *(Equisetum arvense)*. (See *Horsetail* in the chapter on Herbs.)

Cucumbers dislike potatoes, while potatoes grown near cucumbers are more likely to be affected by phytophthora blight, so keep the two apart. Cucumbers also have a dislike for aromatic herbs.

Disease-Resistant Vegetable Varieties

Many vegetable varieties have been specially bred to resist specific plant diseases, and more are constantly being developed.

It's important to know what diseases are most troublesome in your area. Your county's Cooperative Extension Service is a good source of information on this, and may have lists of varieties recommended for local conditions.

Seed catalogs normally indicate which of their offerings have inbred resistance to various problems, often using a code (for instance, "VFT" to show that a tomato cultivar is resistant to verticillium wilt, fusarium wilt, and tobacco mosaic). You can greatly increase your chances of success by heeding this information and matching your choices to the troubles you're most likely to run into.

Eggplant *(Solanum melongena)*

Redroot pigweed makes eggplants more resistant to insect attack. During dry weather, mulching and irrigation will help to prevent wilt disease. Dry cayenne pepper sprinkled on plants while still wet with dew will repel caterpillars. Eggplants growing among green beans will be protected from the Colorado potato beetle. The beetles like eggplant even more than potatoes, but they find the beans repellent.

High-Vitamin Vegetables

A new tomato, 'Doublerich', containing as much vitamin C as citrus fruit, was introduced in 1956. Prof. A. F. Yeager of the University of New Hampshire developed it using crosses of the tiny wild Peruvian tomato, which is four times richer in vitamin C than our ordinary garden types.

A few years later 'Caro-Red', containing about 10 times the amount of vitamin A found in standard varieties, was perfected at the Indiana Experiment Station. 'Caro-Red' owed its richness to its orange pigment, beta-carotene, and a single fruit could supply up to twice the minimum daily requirement of vitamin A for an adult. Perhaps best of all, this was a very delicious tomato to eat. Later came 'Caro-Rich', containing even more vitamin A.

These are just a few examples of the ongoing effort to improve the nutritional content of garden vegetables. Announcements of new vitamin-rich introductions appear in seed catalogs and gardening literature, and those who want the greatest possible food value from their growing space should take note of them.

Horseradish *(Ammoracia rusticana)*

Horseradish and potatoes have a symbiotic effect on each other, causing the potatoes to be healthier and more resistant to disease. Plants should be set at the corners of the potato plot only and should be dug after each season to prevent spreading. Horseradish does not seem to protect against the potato beetle, but it is effective against the blister beetle. A tea made from horseradish is beneficial against monilia on apple trees.

Jerusalem Artichoke *(Helianthus tuberosus)*

In Italy these are called *girasole,* meaning "turn with the sun." They really are a type of sunflower and should not be confused with the globe artichoke, which is an entirely different plant.

Jerusalem artichokes, a native Amerian plant, were known to and used by the Indians. They are a good companion to corn. The tuber is the edible portion, for this sunflower has its surprise at the bottom, the flowers being attractive but not large.

The principal food content of the Jerusalem artichoke is inulin, a tasteless, white polysaccharide dissolved in the sap of the roots, which can be converted into levulose sugar. This is of special interest to diabetics, for levulose is highly nutritious and the sweetest of all known natural sugars. Levulose also occurs in most fruits, in the company of dextrose, which diabetics must avoid, but in the Jerusalem artichoke it is present alone. The artichokes are high in food value and rich in vitamins. They may be cooked or eaten raw in salads.

Kale *(Brassica oleracea acephala)*

This cool-weather crop is fine to grow in the fall garden, and it will stand most average winters if given a little protection.

Kale does well in the same rows as late cabbage or potatoes. If planted about the first of August following late beans or peas, it will continue to grow until a hard freeze. A light freeze does not hurt it and even improves its flavor.

Wild mustard and kale sometimes are a problem in oat fields. Rolling is the best method of control. It should be practiced early in the morning while the plants are still wet with dew. The springy oats will pop back up again, but the mustard or kale will be broken.

Kohlrabi (Brassicaceae)

Kohlrabi is mutually beneficial with onions or beets, with aromatic plants, and surprisingly with cucumbers, in part because they occupy different soil strata. It dislikes strawberries, tomatoes, and pole beans but helps protect the garden members of the mustard family.

It is a demanding plant, needing plenty of water but good drainage, as well as good supplies of compost. It grows best in filtered sunlight.

Leek *(Allium porrum)*

Leek is one of the "heavy feeders" and should be planted in soil well fertilized with rotted manure. Leeks are usually sold in the grocery store (at least where I live) with the root still attached. I once bought several bunches and planted them; they grew well and propagated, and I've had leeks ever since.

Leeks are good plants to grow with celery and onions, and also are benefited by carrots. Returning the favor, leeks repel carrot flies.

Lettuce *(Lactuca sativa)*

In spring I keep a supply of small lettuce plants growing in cold frames. When I pull every other green onion for table use, I pop in lettuce plants. They will aid the onions, and the compost in the onion row will still be in good supply for the lettuce to feed on, while the onion will repel any rabbits.

Lettuce grows well with strawberries, cucumbers, and carrots and it has long been considered good to team with carrots and radishes. Radishes grown with lettuce in summer are particularly succulent.

Lettuce needs cool weather and ample moisture to make its best growth, and I find that the seed will not germinate in very hot weather. Already-started lettuce should have some summer shade.

Melon (Cucurbitaceae)

Crop rotation can be one of your best weapons against garden pests, but do not rotate melon, squash, and cucumber with each other, since all are cucurbits.

Timing is another weapon. Most cucurbits are not very susceptible to borers once they are past the seedling stage, so try either earlier or later plantings. I find that fall-planted cucumbers and squash are almost entirely insect-free.

Do not plant melons near potatoes, though they will grow well with corn and sunflowers. Morning glory is thought to stimulate the germination of melon seeds.

Heavy waxed paper placed under melons helps keep worms from entering, while sabadilla dust is effective, too. (See *Insecticides, Botanical,* in the Pest Control chapter.) Melon leaves, rich in calcium, are good to place on the compost pile.

Okra *(Hibiscus esculentus)*

This native of the Old World tropics is grown for its immature pods, which are called okra or gumbo. It's a warm-weather plant that will grow wherever melons or cucumbers thrive. I plant two rows, dig a trench between, and cover it with mulch. On the north side of my okra I plant a row of sweet bell peppers and on the south side a row of eggplant. All are well mulched as the season advances. When the weather becomes dry, in midsummer, I lay the hose in the trench and flood it so that all three companions grow well.

Onion *(Allium cepa)*

Onions and all members of the Cabbage family get along well with each other. They also like beets, strawberries, tomatoes, lettuce, summer savory, and camomile (sparsely), but do *not* like peas and beans. Ornamental relations of the onion are useful as protective companions for roses.

Since onion maggots travel from plant to plant when set in a row, scatter your onion plants throughout the garden.

Parsley *(Petroselinum hortense)*

Parsley mixed with carrot seed helps to repel carrot flies by its masking aroma. It protects roses against rose beetles. Planted with tomatoes or with asparagus, it will give added vigor to both.

Poultry are sometimes turned loose at intervals in parsley patches where there are many parsley worms, which are the larvae of the black swallowtail butterfly.

A number of different strains of parsley, including the Hamburg *(Petroselinum crispum latifolium),* are grown solely for the fleshy roots, which are cooked and eaten in the same way as parsnips.

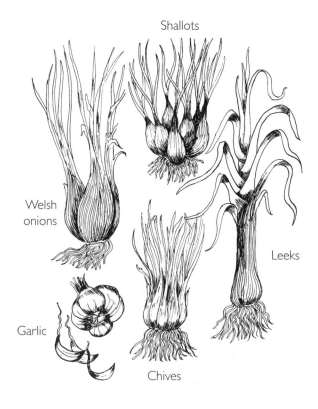

The Onion family is the gardener's best friend.

Parsnip *(Pastinaca sativa)*
The parsnip is of ancient culture, but remains a vegetable for the special palate. The parsnips have few insect enemies and suffer from few diseases, but both the foliage and roots make a safe insect spray. They are not injured by freezing and are often left in the ground over winter. The seeds germinate slowly and unevenly and should not be used if over a year old.

Pea *(Pisum sativum)*
For large crops, treat pea and bean seed with inoculant, a natural bacterial agent available under various brand names from garden centers and seed catalogs. (See *Inoculants* in the Soil Improvement chapter.)

Peas grow well with carrots, turnips, radishes, cucumbers, corn, beans, and potatoes, as well as many aromatic herbs. They do *not* grow well with onions, garlic, and gladiolus.

Always plow pea vines under or return them to the compost pile. Wood ashes used around the base of pea vines help to control aphids.

Peanut *(Arachis hypogaea)*
As members of the Legume family, peanuts are good soil builders. In many areas of the South and Southwest, they may be grown as a second crop after an earlier one, such as carrots or beets, has been harvested. They make a good ground cover in an orchard of young nut trees. (See *Legumes* in the Soil Improvement chapter.)

Pepper, Sweet *(Capsicum frutescens* var. *grossum)*
The general requirements of sweet peppers are surprisingly like those of basil, so plant them together. Sweet peppers also grow well with okra, and since they are very brittle plants, the okra, growing taller, serves as a windbreak.

Pumpkin *(Cucurbita pepo)*
Pumpkins grow well when jimsonweed *(Datura),* sometimes called thorn apple, is in the vicinity. (See the Wild Plants chapter.)

Pumpkins grow well with corn, a practice followed by Native Americans, but pumpkins and potatoes have an inhibiting effect on each other.

Middle Eastern peoples consider the seeds an inexhaustible source of vigor offered by a bountiful nature. While we know today that there are no mysterious potions for tired lovers, we also know that some of the old formulas did perform seeming miracles — not through magic but through good nutrition — and pumpkin seeds are really vitamin-rich.

Pumpkin varieties have been developed with seeds that lack the shell of normal pumpkin and squash. The hull-less seeds may be removed and simply washed and dried; they are a delicious snack when roasted and lightly salted.

Radish *(Raphanus sativus)*

Radish is aided by redroot pigweed, which loosens soil, by nasturtiums, and by mustard's protective oils. Do not rotate radish with cabbage, cauliflower, Brussels sprouts, kohlrabi, broccoli, or turnip, since all are members of the Cabbage family.

Early radishes are good to sow with beets, spinach, carrots, and parsnips to mark the row. Sow radishes with cucumbers, squash, and melons to repel the striped cucumber beetle, and with tomatoes to rout the two-spotted spider mite. Radishes grow well with kohlrabi, bush beans, and pole beans. The presence of leaf lettuce in summer will make radishes more tender. Tobacco dust protects them from flea beetles, and garlic juice from many diseases.

Radish and hyssop should never be sown near each other.

Rhubarb *(Rheum rhaponticum)*

This very ornamental as well as useful plant is a good companion to columbines *(Aquilegia),* helping to protect them against red spider.

Rhubarb leaves contain oxalic acid. They may be boiled in water and made into a spray that, watered into drillings before sowing plants of the Cabbage family, wallflowers, and other seeds, is helpful in preventing clubroot. It is also useful on roses against greenfly and black spot.

Rhubarb stems make delicious pies, but the leaves are very toxic and sometimes also cause skin irritation. They are safe on the compost pile, however.

Rhubarb, often called the pie plant, is technically a vegetable but is mostly used for dessert. It also has been long recognized as a laxative. This is one of our oldest garden plants, which Marco Polo found growing in China centuries ago.

Salsify *(Tragopogon porrifolius)*

Sometimes this is called oyster plant. To achieve a delicate and different flavor, the milky, oyster-flavored roots need a moist, cool soil for at least four months before reaching maturity.

Salsify grows well with mustard greens, and try growing it with watermelons. Plant the warm-weather watermelon several weeks later than the cool-weather salsify. Let the melons fill the middles of the rows before hot, dry weather arrives. Acting as a living mulch and tending to rest on the ground, the melon vines still will leave the salsify foliage exposed to light and air.

Never use salsify seed over a year old.

Shallot *(Allium ascalonicum)*

Shallots, more delicate in flavor than onions, are propagated by planting the sections or cloves that make up the large bulb. They are good to grow with most garden vegetables but, like onions and garlic, should not be located near peas or beans.

Spinach *(Spinacia oleracea)*

Because of its saponin content, spinach is a useful pre-crop and does well planted with strawberries. (See *Saponin* in the Soil Improvement chapter.) *Bacillus thuringiensis* (see Pest Control) may be used as an insect control.

Squash (Curcubitaceae)

Two or three icicle radishes planted in each hill will help prevent insects on squash as on cucumbers. Let the radishes grow and go to seed. Nasturtiums will repel squash bugs and so will cigarette ash and other tobacco residue if placed with the seed when it is planted. Squash planted either earlier or later than usual often will escape insect damage. Here in Oklahoma I find fall-planted squash almost entirely insect-free.

Early in the day, before the sun is strong, squash stinkbugs are sluggish, and in the small garden may be picked off. There also are insect-resistant strains of squash.

Sweet Potato *(Ipomea batalas)*

Sweet potatoes generally have high energy value, only peas and beans yielding more. They have a common enemy, the fungus disease or wilt called stem rot, which can be controlled with disease-free seed and by rotating the crop. White hellebore controls a number of leaf-eating insects. Nematodes can be a problem, and some varieties have been bred with built-in resistance.

If rabbits bother your sweet potato patch, spray with a diluted fish emulsion.

Tomato *(Lycopersicon esculentum)*

Tomatoes and all members of the Brassica (Cabbage) family repel each other and should be kept apart. Tomatoes also dislike potatoes and fennel.

Tomatoes will protect asparagus against the asparagus beetle. Since they are tender plants, put tomatoes in during late spring after the early crop of asparagus spears has been harvested. Tomatoes protect gooseberries against insects.

Tomatoes are compatible with chives, onion, parsley, marigold, nasturtium, and carrot, and for several years I have planted garlic bulbs between my tomato plants to protect them from red spider mites. Stinging nettle growing nearby improves their keeping qualities, and redroot pigweed, in small quantities, is also beneficial.

Though not containing fungicidal elements, tomatoes will protect roses against black spot. The active principle of tomato leaves is solanine, a volatile alkaloid that at one time was used as an agricultural insecticide. To make a spray for roses: Make a solution of tomato leaves in your vegetable juicer, adding four or five pints of water and one tablespoon of cornstarch. Strain and spray on roses where it is not convenient to plant tomatoes as companions. Keep any unused spray refrigerated.

Root excretions of tomatoes have an inhibiting effect on young apricot trees, and don't plant tomatoes near corn, since the tomato fruitworm is identical with the corn earworm. Don't plant near potatoes, either, since tomatoes render them more susceptible to potato blight.

Unlike most other vegetables, tomatoes prefer to grow in the same place year after year. This is all right unless you have a disease problem, in which case plant your tomatoes in a new area. Since they are heavy feeders, give them ample quantities of compost or decomposed manure. Mulch and water in dry weather to maintain soil moisture and stave off wilt disease and blossom end rot. But never water tomatoes from the top. Water from below and water deeply.

If you smoke, be sure to wash your hands thoroughly before you work in your garden, for tomatoes are susceptible to diseases transmitted through tobacco.

Turnip-Rutabaga (*Brassica rapa* and *Brassica napobrassica*)
An accident revealed that hairy vetch and turnips are excellent

companions. Turnip seeds became mixed with the vetch that a gardener planted, and they came up as volunteer plants. He found that the turnip greens were completely free of the aphids that usually infest them, apparently because the vetch provided shelter for ladybugs, which feast on aphids. Elsewhere it has been found that wood ashes around the base of turnip plants will control scab.

I find that peas planted near turnips are mutually benefited. Turnip and radish seed mixed with clover will bolster the nitrogen content of the soil. In your crop rotation it is good to follow the heavy feeders with light feeders such as turnips and rutabagas.

Turnips dislike hedge mustard and knotweed, and do not rotate them with other members of the Cabbage family such as broccoli and kohlrabi. A naturally occurring chemical compound in turnips when synthesized is deadly to aphids, spider mites, houseflies, German cockroaches, and bean beetles.

Rutabagas take much the same culture as turnips but require a longer growing season.

Watermelon *(Citrullus vulgaris)*

Watermelons are good to interplant with potatoes, particularly if the potatoes are mulched with straw. The hybrid seedless watermelons, which set no pollen, will produce better if planted with a good pollinator such as 'Sugar Baby'. Watermelons need plenty of sunshine, so do not plant them with or near tall-growing vegetables.

Herbs

Absinthium *(Artemisia absinthium)*
Also called wormwood, this plant is grown as a border to keep animals from the garden. Ornamental species such as *A. pontica* have leaves of great delicacy and are good to plant in flower beds and around choice evergreens. (See *Wormwood.*)

Aloe Vera *(Aloe barbadensis)*
Nature's own medicine plant, known and used for centuries, is a vegetable belonging to the Lily family. The name "aloe vera" means "true aloe," and it is so named because, among 200 species of aloe, it has the best medicinal properties.

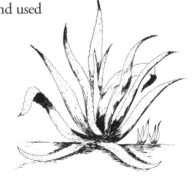

The aloe genus belongs to a larger class of plants known as the xeroids, which possess the ability to close their stomata completely to avoid the loss of water. The plants are easy to grow outside in warm, frost-free climates, and equally easy to grow indoors in pots. Possibly because of the bitter taste of the gel, they appear to be completely disease- and

Aloe vera is known as nature's medicine plant.

insect-free. Almost all xeroids are laxative in nature and have a bitter flavor.

Aloin is the thick, mucilaginous yellow juice that occurs at the base of the aloe leaf, and is also present in the rind. The gel may be removed from the leaf as one would fillet a fish. It is a very slippery, clear, viscous juice useful for sunburns and for healing cutaneous ulcers of radioactive origin, as well as burns and scalds of various types. Many fishermen carry aloe vera aboard their boats to stop the pain of a sting from a Portuguese man-of-war. It also will stop the sting often experienced when gathering okra.

The gel may be used instead of tree wound dressing if it becomes necessary to cut a tree limb. The surface will heal over quickly and insects are repelled by the bitter taste. The juice may be mixed with water to make a spray for plants. Powdered aloes dusted on young plants will repel rabbits, but this must be repeated after rain. Aloe vera plants, thrown in the drinking water for chickens, are said to cure them of certain diseases.

Anise *(Pimpinella anisum)*

The spicy seeds of this annual herb, related to caraway and dill, are used to flavor licorice as well as pastry, cookies, and certain kinds of cheese. The oil extracted from the seeds is used to make absinthe, and it is also used in medicine. The flower, powdered and infused with vermouth, is used for flavoring muscatel wine. Anise is antiseptic, and is useful as an ointment (when mixed with lard) for lice and itching from insect bites.

When sown with coriander, aniseed will germinate better, grow more vigorously, and form better heads.

Basil *(Ocimum basilicum)*

Basil helps tomatoes to overcome both insects and disease, also improving growth and flavor. Since this is a small plant, one to two feet tall, grow it parallel to the tomatoes rather than among them. It repels mosquitoes and flies, and when laid over tomatoes in a serving bowl will deter fruit flies.

Sweet basil has inch-long, dark green leaves and a clove-pepperish odor and taste. Pinch out the plant tops and they will grow into little bushes, the dwarf varieties especially becoming beautifully compact. As a kitchen herb, basil is used in vinegar, soup, stew, salad, chopped meat, and sausage, as well as in cottage cheese, egg, and tomato dishes, and may be sprinkled over vegetables. 'Dark Opal' makes a very handsome houseplant.

Though it is often said that herbs enhance everything except dessert, sweet basil is one that may be used to give a subtle, indefinable, but delicious flavor to pound cake. It is also one of the culinary herbs that may be used in certain dishes to replace black pepper. (See *Pepper Substitutes* in this chapter.)

It has been known since ancient times that basil and rue dislike each other intensely. Perhaps this is because basil is sweet and rue is very bitter.

Bay *(Lauris nobilis)*
Bay (or laurel) leaves put in stored grains such as wheat, rice, rye, beans, oats, and corn will eliminate weevils. The bay belongs to the same family as the cinnamon, camphor, avocado, and sassafras trees. I have tried sassafras leaves in grains and flours and find them also effective against insects and weevils.

Bee Balm *(Monarda)*
This plant improves both the growth and flavor of tomatoes.

Borage (Boraginaceae)
This is an excellent provider of organic potassium, calcium, and other natural minerals of benefit to plants. Grow this herb in orchards and as a border for strawberry beds. Honeybees like to feast on the blossoms.

Borage

Camomile *(Chamomile)*

The real plant, the German or wild camomile *(Matricaria chamomilla)*, recognizable by the hollow bottom of the blossom and its highly aromatic odor, often is confused with Roman camomile *(Anthemis nobilis)*. This is an excellent companion to cabbages and onions, improving growth and flavor of both. But it should be grown sparingly, only one plant every 150 feet.

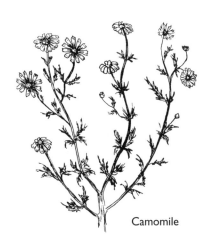

Camomile

Wheat grown with camomile in the proportion of 100 to 1 will grow heavier and with fuller ears, but too much will harm field crops.

Camomile contains the substance chamazulene, which has anti-allergic and anti-inflammatory properties when used in the form of tea. It is also used for diarrhea or scour in calves. A tea of one-third each camomile, lemon balm, and chervil applied as a warm compress will cure hoof rot in animals.

Camomile flowers may be used in the dog's bed against fleas. When using herbs in pet pillows, simply add the dried form to the stuffing, occasionally adding more to freshen up.

The blossoms soaked in cold water for a day or two can be used as a spray for treating many plant diseases and to control damping-off in greenhouses and cold frames.

A camomile rinse is excellent for blond hair. Use three or four tablespoons of dried flowers to a pint of water. Boil twenty to thirty minutes, straining when cool. Shampoo the hair before using, since it must be free of oil. Pour rinse over the hair several times and do not rinse with clear water after using. It will leave the hair smelling like sweet clover.

Camomile contains a hormone that stimulates the growth of yeast. Grown with peppermint in very small quantities, it increases the essential oil.

Caraway *(Carum carvi)*

Since it is difficult to sprout caraway seed, sow it with a companion crop of peas. After harvesting the peas, harrow the area and the caraway will come up. It's good to plant on wet, heavy land, the long roots making an excellent substitute for subsoiling. Do not grow fennel near it.

Europeans like and use caraway seed more than we do. It is put in rye bread for its aromatic flavor and to make it more digestible. It is also used in cakes, cheeses, and apple and cabbage recipes.

Catnip *(Nepeta cataria)*

Catnip contains an insect-repellent oil, nepetalactone, and fresh catnip steeped in water and sprinkled on plants will send flea beetles scurrying.

The catnip compound is chemically allied to those found in certain insects. Two of these occur in ants and another in the walkingstick insect, which ejects a spray against such predators as ants, beetles, spiders, birds, and even humans. Freshly picked catnip placed on infected shelves will drive away black ants. But my cats love catnip, and I like to eat it in salads.

Chervil *(Anthriscus cerefolium)*

This is one of the few herbs that will grow better in partial shade, which can be provided by taller plants growing near it. It does not take kindly to transplanting. Chervil is a good companion to radishes, improving their growth and flavor.

Chive *(Allium schoenoprausum)*

Chives are a good companion to carrots, improving both growth and flavor. Planted in apple orchards they are of benefit in preventing apple scab, or made into chive tea may be used as a spray for apple scab or against powdery mildew on gooseberries and cucumbers.

Coffee Substitutes

The price of America's favorite hot brew fluctuates from one year to the next depending on weather conditions in the countries where it is grown. It is interesting to know that there are a number of herbal substitutes that can be made into an acceptable hot drink and are almost universally available. Like any food or beverage, however, the product should be weighed on its own merits. To taste parched and perked seeds, roots, or nuts with the thought of "coffee" in mind is unfair to the substitute.

Chicory

Chicory (Cichorium intybus), which grows on roadsides and in waste clay soils from Canada southward, is identifiable when young by its leaves, which resemble those of the dandelion. But as the plants mature, a rigid, loosely branched 2-foot stem develops, and blue flowers bloom in midsummer. The tubular roots, which grow horizontally, should be dug in September after flowering is over. To use chicory as a substitute or as a coffee additive, the roots should be washed, coarsely ground, dried in a very slow oven for two or three hours, then roasted in a clean skillet. This should be done very slowly and the granulated chicory repeatedly stirred until the proper color and flavor are reached.

Chicory does not taste like coffee, but when used as an additive, some people believe, it improves the color and flavor of South American coffee, as well as extending the number of cups. In France, and in our own South, subject to French influence, chicory is added to coffee, not as an adulterant but for its distinctive flavor.

According to Virginia Scully in *A Treasury of American Indian Herbs,* the Native Americans roasted the roots and used them as they did the dandelion roots. Nelson Coon, author of *Using Plants for Healing,* writes of chicory as "a plant of ancient usage," the name tracing back through Arab medicinal language to Greek and Egyptian, and mention of the use of chicory is found in Roman writings.

Cleavers (Galium sparine), after chicory, seems to be the most popular coffee substitute. Cleavers grows in Alaska, southward across Canada, and on down into Texas, and is found on seashores and in rocky woods. Although cleavers sprouts may be eaten in the spring, the tiny twin burr-seeds ripen later. Cleavers grows best in damp thickets. Cleavers, also known as goose grass, is eagerly sought by animals and poultry for its medicinal qualities. Cleavers also, according to all the old herbalists, has a reputation as a reducing diet par excellence, painlessly paring pounds from plump persons.

The usefulness of cleavers is not confined to its value as a reducing diet or as a palatable cooked vegetable. According to Euell Gibbons in *Stalking the Healthful Herbs,* the little two-lobed seeds make the best coffee substitute of almost any plant growing in our range. Perhaps this is because cleavers belongs to the Rubiaceae, the natural order of plants to which the coffee tree also belongs.

The little hard fruits should be gathered during the summer when they are full-sized and roasted in an oven until they are very brown. They can then be made into a beverage that tastes much like coffee and also has a definite coffee aroma. Cleavers contains no caffeine.

Cleavers has long been considered a medicinal herb, its properties being listed as diuretic, tonic, alterative, and somewhat laxative. Gather the herb in May or June when in flower and dry in a warm room.

Nut grass (Cyperus esculentus) is an herb of almost universal distribution. If nut grass tubers are roasted until they are a very dark brown all through, then pulverized in a blender or coffee mill, they make a very palatable hot drink when brewed exactly as you do coffee. Nut grass coffee contains no harmful stimulants and can freely be given to children who insist on having "coffee" when the grown-ups do.

Sunflower (Helianthus annus) has long been used by Native Americans, who parched the highly nutritious seeds and made them into a meal for gruel and cakes. Frequently, they added water to the meal as a drink, and crushed roasted seeds to make a drink like coffee.

Sassafras (Sassafras albidum and *Sassafras varifolium)* is also called wild cinnamon or mitten plant. It likes to grow in rich woods in humusy soil and both leaves and bark may be used, the leaves being gathered in the spring and the bark in the fall. The name sassafras is a corruption of the Spanish word *saxifrage,* which in turn is derived from two Latin words, *saxum,* meaning "a rock," and *frango,* meaning "I break." It is interesting to note that herbalists recommend to those suffering with stones in the kidneys and other kidney diseases that sassafras be always included in a formula of kidney-stimulating herbs.

A hot drink of sassafras may be prepared by stirring a half teaspoonful of the ground bark in a cup of boiling water. Cover with a saucer for about five minutes. Stir, strain, and add a little honey for sweetness.

Dandelion roots (Taraxacum officinale), roasted, have long been used as a coffee substitute and taste much like chicory. The young leaves often appear in salads, and the Native Americans chewed the young stems like gum.

Dried persimmon seeds (Diospyros), **wild senna seeds** *(Cassia occidentalis),* and **roasted acorn beans** have been ground and used as coffee. The black or red-oak *(Quercus)* acorns were used.

Cereals, nuts, peas, soya beans, and even okra seeds have been roasted and used as coffee substitutes, dilutants (thinners), or additives. Again, when it comes to extending the family coffee supply, it is well to remember that some sacrifice of flavor must be made.

Comfrey *(Symphytum officinale)*

Comfrey, also called knitbone or healing herb, is high in calcium, potassium, and phosphorus, and rich in vitamins A and C. It was an ancient belief that comfrey preparations taken internally or as a poultice bound to injured parts hastened the healing of broken bones.

It is possible that the nutrients present in comfrey actually do assist in the healing process, since we now know that the herb also contains a drug called allantoin, which promotes the strengthening of the lining of hollow internal organs. However, this herb also contains alkaloids that cause liver damage and is no longer considered safe for internal use.

The leaves of Russian comfrey are ideal for the compost heap, having a carbon-nitrogen ratio similar to that of barnyard manure.

Coriander *(Coriandrum sativum)*

Coriander has a reputation for repelling aphids while being immune to them itself. It helps anise to germinate but hinders the seed formation of fennel. In blossom the herb is very attractive to bees.

Many people think the foliage and fresh seed of coriander have a disagreeable smell, but as the seeds ripen they gain a delicious fragrance that intensifies as they dry. The savory seeds, sometimes sugar-coated as a confection, are baked in breads or used to flavor meats.

Coriander has four times more carotene than parsley, three times as much calcium, more protein and minerals, more riboflavin, and more vitamin B_1 and niacin. Oil of coriander is used medicinally to correct nausea.

Dill *(Anethum graveolens)*

Dill is a good companion to cabbage, improving its growth and health. It does not do well by carrots and if allowed to mature will greatly reduce that crop, so pull it before it blooms.

Dill will do well if sowed in empty spaces where early beets have been harvested, and light sowings may be made with lettuce, onions, or cucumbers. Honeybees like to visit dill blossoms.

Drying Herbs

Leaf herbs should be cut, washed, tied in loose bunches, and allowed to drip dry. Place upside down in large brown paper bags that have been labeled. Close the mouth of the bag about the stems; let the herbs hang free inside the bag. Hang the bags where they will have good air circulation. In this way none of the oil is absorbed by contact with the paper, as may be the case if dried herbs are stored in cardboard boxes.

With seed herbs, let the plants mature until the ripe seeds part from the dry umbels with a little pressure. This occurs after they

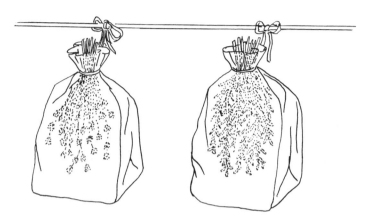

Dry herbs in paper bags hung in an airy place.

lose their greenish color but before they will drop of their own accord. Cut the heads on a dry morning and spread them out on brown paper in the sun for the rest of the day, stirring occasionally. Do this for several days, taking them in at night, until they are thoroughly dry. Seeds may be stored in opaque glass bottles or clear ones away from the light.

Elecampane *(Inula helenium)*

My German heritage bids me have great respect for elecampane, sometime called horseheal or horse alder. This herb was under the protection of the goddess Hulda, who first taught mortals the art of spinning and weaving flax. Candied elecampane, according to a 17th-century herbal, was thought to "cause mirth."

Elecampane came to America as a healer, being introduced into gardens as a home remedy. Finding the climate congenial, it went native and now grows wild in many places.

The substance most abundantly contained in elecampane root is inulin, a sort of invert starch usable as a replacement for ordinary starch in the diet of diabetics. It also contains a volatile oil and several identifiable crystalline substances. The thick, yellow taproot has the odor of camphor.

Elecampane once was used in England for the heaves in horses.

As far back as 1885 a Dr. Korab demonstrated that the active bitter principle of the plant, called helenin, was a powerful antiseptic and bactericide, particularly destructive to the tubercle bacillus.

Elecampane in the garden provides a six-foot-tall accent of bright yellow in midsummer when the large-rayed flowers stand above the enormous felty leaves. The plants are useful in providing a bit of shade for lower-growing mints.

Fennel *(Nigella sativa)*

Most plants dislike fennel, and it is one herb that should be planted well away from the vegetable garden, since it has an inhibiting effect on bush beans, caraway, kohlrabi, and tomatoes. Fennel planted away from the garden is valuable for its masses of fringed foliage. At one time the fragrant seeds, which smell and taste like licorice, were made into a tea soothing to colicky babies. Mixed with peppermint leaves, it also makes a delicious tea for adults. Fennel is inhibited by the presence of coriander and will not form seed. It also dislikes wormwood.

Garlic *(Allium sativum)*

The Babylonians and Hindus knew of garlic's medicinal power 3,000 years ago, and it was well known to the ancient Egyptians, who fed great quantities of garlic to the workers who built the pyramids. The Greek physicians, fathers of present-day medicine, used garlic in their prescriptions, and it was rationed to the soldiers of the mighty Roman armies.

The 800-year-old medical school of Salerno included garlic in its *materia medica,* and it always has been one of the standbys of folk medicine practitioners.

Garlic is an effective control for many insects. Try this recipe for garden use: Take three to four ounces of chopped garlic bulbs and soak in two tablespoons of mineral oil for a day. Add one pint of water in which one teaspoon of fish emulsion has been dissolved. Stir well. Strain the liquid and store in a glass or china container, as it reacts with metals. Dilute this, starting with one part to 20 parts of water, and use as a spray against your worst insect pests.

If sweet potatoes or other garden plants are attracting rabbits, try this spray. Rabbits dislike the smell of fish, too, so fish emulsion may help.

Garlic sprays are useful in controlling late blight on tomatoes and potatoes. Garlic is an effective destroyer of the diseases that damage stone fruits, cucumbers, radishes, spinach, beans, nuts, and tomatoes.

A garlic-based oil sprayed on breeding ponds showed a 100 percent kill of mosquito larvae in a University of California experiment. Garlic cloves stored in the grain are good against grain weevils.

Garlic grown in a circle around fruit trees is good against borers. It is beneficial to the growth of vetch and is protective planted with roses. All alliums, however, inhibit the growth of peas and beans. Plant garlic with tomatoes against red spider. I have done this for three successive years with good results.

Herbs for Tea

Herb teas have both aided digestion and given pleasure to untold generations. Here is how to make tea:

Pick some of the leaves, using only those undamaged (or dried leaves may be used). You will need four or five leaves for a cup of tea and about a handful for a pot. Wash the leaves in cool water, put in a cup or pot, and pour boiling water over them. Let steep, covered, for three to five minutes. Add sugar or honey to sweeten.

Please note: Research on herbs is ongoing, and some that were formerly used internally are now thought to be potentially harmful. Make teas only from plants suggested for this purpose in up-to-date guides to the use of herbs.

Horehound *(Marrubian vulgare)*

In centuries past, virtues attributed to horehound included the power to cure snakebite and merit as a fly repellent, vermifuge, and an ointment for wounds and itches. The Hebrew name for the plant, *marrob,* means "a bitter juice." It was one of the five bitter herbs required to be eaten at the Passover feast. The Romans considered it a good and sometimes magical herb. Horehound's real value relates to pulmonary ailments and it is widely used as an ingredient in lozenges for coughs and colds.

For small stems and better quality, grow the plants intended for candy making close together. Either the fresh or dried herb can be used for this purpose.

Grasshoppers and other insects dislike the taste of horehound. The plant grows well with tomatoes, improving their quality, causing them to bear more abundantly and continue later in the season.

Horsetail
See the Wild Plants chapter.

Hyssop *(Hyssopus officinalis)*
It's hard to find anything more delightful than a hyssop hedge in full sun. The blue, white, and pink flowered hyssop makes an intriguing design grown with gray Roman wormwood.

Sow the hyssop seeds in late fall so they will germinate first thing in the spring. Planted near grapevines they will increase their yield,

---

FRECKLE REMEDIES

I do not dislike freckles — my mother always told me they were the scars left by the angels' kisses — but some lucky people seem to receive more kisses than they want. If freckles trouble you, elder flowers added to facial steam baths will clear and soften the skin, and are also good against freckles and faulty pigmentation, especially when they are used in conjunction with whey and yogurt. Such face packs are not only soothing but also tonic and stimulating. Parsley water externally used also is said to remove freckles or moles.

Freshly crushed leaves or freshly pressed juice of lady's-mantle *(Alchemilla vulgaris)* is helpful against inflammation of the skin and acne, as well as freckles. Externally used, lime flowers *(Tilia)* are a fine cosmetic against freckles, wrinkles, and impurities of the skin, and they also are stimulating to hair growth.

and near cabbages will lure away the cabbage butterfly. Bees are very fond of visiting hyssop blossoms, yet many other insects find the plant repellent. Radishes will not do well if hyssop is nearby.

Hyssop leaves have a peculiar fragrance reminiscent of civet, yet some use them the same way as savory. A compress of hyssop leaves is good for removing black and blue spots from bruises.

This is another of the bitter herbs used in Jewish ceremonies but it is not the true hyssop of the Bible, which is believed to be a species of origanum.

Lavender *(Lavendula officinalis)*

In a 2 percent emulsion spray for cotton pests, lavender kills somewhere between 50 to 80 percent within a period of 24 hours.

Few ticks are found in lavender plantations, although neighboring woods and shrubs may harbor many. It has been used effectively as a mouse repellent, and lavender sachets are often put in woolen clothing to repel moths, while leaves scattered under woolen carpets are helpful for the same purpose.

The plant grows from seed very slowly. Both plants and seeds are obtainable from Nichols Garden Nursery. (See Sources.)

Lemon Balm *(Melissa officinalis)*

Lemon balm, often called the bee herb, has long been famous for its delightful, lemon-scented foliage and honeyed sweetness. *Melissa,* the generic name, is Greek for "honeybee," and there is a very old belief that bees will not leave the hive area if melissa grows near it. Pliny wrote, "When bees have stayed away they do find their way back home by it."

Melissa tea calms the nervous system and stimulates the heart, it is very relaxing, and may even dispel headache or migraine. In pastures this plant increases the flow of cows' milk, and it is very good to give cows after calving in a tea with marjoram.

Lovage *(Levisticum officinale)*

Lovage planted here and there will improve the health and flavor of other plants. It is one of the herbs that may be used to reduce the amount of salt used for seasoning and is delicious sprinkled on salads or used in cheese biscuits. In dishes that need strengthening, it can replace meat stock and is excellent in soups and casseroles.

Lovage will winter well, but in colder climates the roots should have some protection.

Marjoram *(Marjorana hortensis)*

This small, easily grown plant is probably one of the oldest herbs in use. "Marjoram" really covers three very different kinds of marjoram, all of which belong to the Labiatae family.

The sweet marjoram, an annual, is the most popular for flavoring, especially in sausages. It was used extensively by the Greeks, who gave it the name that means "joy of the mountains." Its disinfectant and preserving qualities made it an invaluable culinary herb in the Middle Ages.

Pot marjoram is a perennial with a bit less flavor but more easily grown.

Wild marjoram *(Oregano vulgare)* is a wild as well as a cultivated variety with a strong flavor, the pungency varying according to where it grows. This herb, also known as oregano, is used the world over in Italian, Mexican, and Spanish dishes, and is believed to have both stimulating and medicinal properties, since it contains thymol, a powerful antiseptic when used internally or externally. The whole plant of oregano is covered with hairy oil glands. The pleasant aromatic scent, reminiscent of thyme, is very lasting — even the dead leaves and stems retain it during the winter or when dried for culinary use.

In the garden all the marjorams have a beneficial effect on nearby plants, improving both growth and flavor.

Mint

Mint *(Mentha)*

Mint is a good companion to cabbage and tomatoes, improving their health and flavor. Both mint and tomatoes are strengthened in the vicinity of stinging nettle. Mints such as apple, orange, and pineapple will thrive under English walnut trees, in part because of the filtered sunlight.

Mint deters the white cabbageworm by repelling the egg-laying butterflies. Spearmint repels ants and may help to keep aphids off nearby plants. (See also *Peppermint* and *Spearmint.*)

Mint is a repellent against clothes moths when used indoors, and is useful against black flea beetles. The leaves strewn under rabbit cages will keep flies to a minimum, while dried leaves (or mint oils) will repel rats and mice.

Mugwort *(Artemisia vulgaris lactiflora)*

Mugwort is one of the most useful members of the Artemisia family. Planted in chicken yards it will help repel lice, and since the chickens like it as a food, it is also thought to be helpful in ridding them of worms. Made into a weak tea, it may be used as a fruit tree spray.

Mugwort is not good too near other garden plants because it has a growth-retarding effect, particularly in years of heavy rainfall. The roots and leaves exude a toxic substance. This soluble toxic, absinthin, washed off by rain, soaks into the soil near the plant and remains active over an indefinite period of time.

Orach *(Atriplex hortensis)*

This beautiful annual, sometimes called French spinach, has shield-shaped, wavy leaves of beet red. They have a mealy texture similar to its close relative, lamb's-quarters, and are also used as a potherb. While orach may be planted in the garden, it should never be placed near potatoes, since it has an inhibiting effect on their growth.

Old-time herbalists believe that orach had a cleansing quality either raw or cooked and if laid upon swollen glands of the throat would cure the condition.

Oregano *(Origanum vulgare)*

Sow with broccoli to repel the cabbage butterfly. (See *Marjoram.*)

Pennyroyal *(Mentha pulegium)*

Plant this with broccoli, Brussels sprouts, and cabbage against cabbage maggot. Like tansy, it may be grown at doorways to repel ants, and is also a good mosquito repellent if rubbed on the skin. Fresh or dried sprigs have long been used as a flea repellent.

Pepper Substitutes

Basil, summer savory, thyme, marjoram, and nasturtium can help replace pepper in cooking for those who have digestive disturbances.

Peppermint *(Mentha piperita)*

Of all herbs, this makes the greatest demand on the soil for humus and moisture. It will benefit from a small amount of chicken manure if well broken down.

Peppermint drives away red ants from shrubs, and planted among cabbage it will repel the white cabbage butterfly. When growing with camomile it will have less oil, but the camomile will benefit and have more. The oil of peppermint is increased when it is grown with stinging nettle.

Black mint is distinguished from other species by purple stems and dark green leaves. It grows about three feet tall and is crowned with spikes of lavender flowers in midsummer. It is widely used for medicinal and commercial purposes. (See also *Mint* and *Spearmint*.)

Rue *(Ruta graveolens)*

By now I'm sure everybody knows that rue doesn't like basil. But an authority as ancient as Pliny tells us that "rue and the fig tree are in great league and amitie together."

Rue planted near roses or raspberries will deter the Japanese beetle. It can be clipped and made into an attractive hedge, but first be sure you are not allergic to it, since the foliage can cause dermatitis as severe as that from poison ivy when the plant is coming into flower. The intensity of the eruption seems aggravated by the presence of sunlight. If you happen to be perspiring and working bare-handed with rue, you may get poisoned. If this happens, washing with brown soap or covering the exposed area with oil will help.

Rue may be grown among flowers as well as vegetables, where its good looks will add to the planting. It is protective to many trees and shrubs. It is good near manure piles and around barns for discouraging both house and stable flies.

The ancient Schola Salernitans wrote that "Rue putteth fleas to flight." However, it should be used only for dog pillows or beds, for cats do not like it. Anything rubbed with the leaves of rue will be free from cats' depredations — good to know if your house cats tend to claw the furniture.

Sage *(Salvia officinalis)*

Sage is protective to cabbages and all their relatives against the white cabbage butterfly, and it also makes the cabbage plants more succulent and tasty.

The herb also is good to grow with carrots, protecting them against the carrot fly, and is mutually beneficial with rosemary. Do not plant sage with cucumber, which does not like aromatic herbs in general and sage in particular.

Originally sage was used medicinally in stuffing and meats to make them more digestible, but we have grown to like the flavor. It has often been made into a tea, but is now considered harmful if much is taken internally.

Salt Substitutes

The clever use of herbs can replace salt in many dishes and reduce the amount needed in others. Those on a salt-free diet can flavor their food deliciously by using such herbs as celery, summer savory, thyme, lovage, and marjoram.

Santolina (*Chamaecyparis* spp.)

This South European plant, sometimes called lavender cotton, is a good moth repellent. The name is from *sanctum linum,* meaning "holy flax." The plants are improved by being pruned as soon as the blossoms fall.

Savory, Summer *(Satureia hortensis)*
In Germany savory is called the bean herb because it's good to grow with beans and also to cook with them. It goes with onions as well, improving both growth and flavor.

Savory, Winter *(Satureia montana)*
Winter savory is a subshrub about 15 inches tall. Its leaves, though not as delicate as summer savory, may be used in cooking. It is useful as an insect repellent, too.

Sesame *(Sesamum orientale)*
Sesame is an herb grown in tropical countries, mainly for the oil obtained from its seeds. The oil is used in salad dressings and for cooking, while the delicious seeds are used to flavor bread, candy, biscuits, and other delicacies. Sesamin is derived from sesame oil and is used as a synergist to strengthen the effect of pyrethrum.
Sesame is very sensitive to root exudates from sorghum *(Andropogon sorghum)* and will not ripen well when grown near it.

Southernwood *(Artemisia abrotanum)*
Dry the leaves of southernwood, place them in nylon net bags, and hang them in the closet to prevent moths. Burned to ashes in the fireplace, they will remove any cooking odors from the house.
Southernwood has green, finely divided leaves with a lemon-mixed-with-pine scent. Grown near cabbages, it will protect them from cabbageworm butterfly and near fruit trees will repel fruit tree moths. Among its names are old man, lad's love, and even maiden's ruin!

Spearmint *(Mentha spicata)*
Spearmint also is called green mint, pea mint, and lamb mint. (See *Mint.*)

Sugar Substitutes
Three herbs that can reduce the use of sugar in cooking and sweets are lemon balm, sweet cicely, and angelica. They are

particularly good in tart fruit or fruit pies made of black currant, red currant, rhubarb, gooseberry, plums, and tart apples. Not only do these herbs make it possible to use sometimes half the usual quantity of sugar, but they also impart a delicious flavor. Chopped sweet cicely may be added to lightly sugared strawberries.

Sweet Basil *(Ocimum basilicum)*
See *Basil*.

Tarragon, French *(Artemisia dracunculus)*
Use potato fertilizer as a side dressing for tarragon in the spring and again right after the first cutting to increase the vitality of the plant. To reset tarragon successfully, the roots must be carefully untangled. Each section of root eased apart from the clump may be reset to form another plant. This is best done every third year in March or early April. As a cooking herb tarragon is something very special, and it is particularly good for flavoring vinegar.

Thyme *(Thymus vulgaris)*
Thyme has an ancient history as a medicinal and culinary herb. The oil still is used as the basis of a patent cough medicine, while thymol has antibacterial powers of considerable importance. But thyme is of value mainly in cooking, being very good for poultry seasoning and dressing. Lemon thyme makes a delicious herbal tea.

The herb deters the cabbageworm and is good planted anywhere in the garden, accenting the aromatic qualities of other plants and herbs.

Valerian *(Valeriana officinalis)*
This herb is good anywhere in the garden, particularly to give vegetables added vigor. It is rich in phosphorus and stimulates phosphorus activity where grown; it is attractive to earthworms and therefore particularly useful in the compost pile.

It is thought that the Pied Piper of Hamelin used valerian to clear the town of rats, yet many gardeners find it attracts cats, which love to nibble the leaves and roll aginst them. The *Universal*

Herbal of 1820 states: "It is well known that cats are very fond of the roots of valerian; rats are equally partial to it — hence rat-catchers employ them to draw the vermin together."

Valerian enjoyed great prominence in colonial days as a drug plant, the strangely scented root being brewed into a sedative tea. Since the oil of valerian does have an effect on the central nervous system, the tea should not be drunk often.

Cold tea is made by this rule: Put one level teaspoon crushed dried valerian root to soak in one cup cold water. Cover and place in a cold place for 12 to 24 hours. Strain and drink about one hour before retiring.

Woodruff, Sweet *(Asperula odorata)*

Sweet woodruff is an excellent ground cover, particularly under crab apple trees. While it will grow in the sun, the foliage is darker green and much more abundant if it receives shade at least half of the day.

Wormwood *(Artemisia absinthium)*

This herb, particularly the variety *cineraria,* will keep animals out of the garden when used as a border. It's a good repellent for moths, flea beetles, and cabbageworm but-terfly. It discourages slugs if sprayed on the ground. Fleas on cats and dogs may be dis-lodged with a bath of wormwood tea.

Wormwood

Many artemisias are of value as orna-mentals, their cool, silvery beauty pro-viding a fine contrast for flowers, such as red geraniums, of brilliant color. They do not attract honeybees, but small wasps seem to be frequent visitors. Keep worm-wood out of the garden since most plants growing near it do not do well, particularly anise, caraway, fennel, and sage.

Wild Plants

Algae

Here is a food source, not yet fully explored, that may prove of great value as populations increase, for the total amount of photosynthesis carried on by marine algae may be ten times greater than the total of such activity in all land plants. If this is true, then we may well look to the plants of the sea as a rich, abundant, and relatively untapped source of foodstuffs.

In some parts of the world, for example Japan and China, algae have for many years been important items in the human diet. Farmers in many coastal regions cultivate brown algae on bamboo stems pushed into the ocean bottom in shallow waters. Dried preparations of these brown algae, available in many food stores in the United States, are very rich in minerals and also have moderate quantities of carbohydrates and vitamins.

Brown algae, because of their rich mineral content, also are often used as soil fertilizers (spread on fields and plowed under), or they may be dried and burned and their ash used as fertilizer. Some species are a commercial source of iodine for medicinal use.

Amaranth *(Amaranthus retroflexus)*

This plant, sometimes called rough pigweed and commonly found

in disturbed ground everywhere, is one of the best
weeds for pumping nutrients
from the subsoil.

Amaranth

Amaranth loosens the
soil for such crops as carrot,
radish, and beet. It helps
potatoes yield more abun-
dantly and is good to grow
with onions, corn, pepper,
and eggplant — but keep it
thinned. Tomatoes grown
with the weed are more resistant to insect attack.

Euell Gibbons says in his
Stalking the Healthful Herbs
that green amaranth has a
higher iron content than any other green vegetable except parsley.

A type of amaranth grown widely in rural Mexico is known as
"the sacred food of the Aztecs." The small seeds, easily threshed
from the large heads, can be baked with bread. Sometimes they are
even popped, mixed with honey, and eaten as a confection. In
India certain species are eaten as a salad or cooked like spinach,
and the seed is ground into flour.

Amaranth (which is distantly related to beets) has a higher protein content than the cultivated beet, is higher in vitamin C, and
has approximately the same amount of vitamin A.

Aster *(Asteroides)*

Many asters are soil indicators. Some like low, moist soil, so if
the bushy type *(Boltonia asteroides)* or the purple-stemmed aster
(A. puniceus) shows up in your pastures or fields, it indicates a
need for drainage. The sea aster *(A. tripolium)* grows on seasides
and near salt mines and is a salt and soda collector. The poisonous woody aster *(Xylorhiza parryi)* of the West indicates an
alkaline soil.

Baked-appleberry *(Rubus chamaemorus)*
Most of us are familiar with the blackberry-dewberry family, Rubus, but one member has been neglected. The baked-appleberry, or cloudberry, is found growing in wet areas in acid peats from the Arctic regions southwest through New England. It bears a single, soft, pinkish berry, which grows on a 12-inch stem bearing a few scalloped leaves. The berries make a delicious fresh dessert, and may be preserved in jams or prepared as juice.

Broom Bush *(Sarothamnus vulgaris)*
This useful weed grows on the poorest, stoniest soils and those that are sandy and slightly to medium acid. Being rich in calcium carbonate, the plant improves the soil through decomposition of its leaves and stems. In a thin stand it will provide shelter for young tree seedlings, but it will choke them out if too many of the weeds are present.

Burdock *(Arctium)*
Do not allow wild burdocks to grow, since they are robbers of the soil. Particularly do not allow them to go to seed, for the burrs will adhere to the hair of sheep, horses, and dogs, even clothing, and be spread far and wide.

Burdock roots have medicinal value and are said to alleviate gout and skin diseases. An edible burdock ('Takinogawa') has been developed in Japan, where the cooked roots are greatly relished for their refreshing, pungent flavor. The Japanese also value this burdock for its reputed blood-purifying qualities and the relief it is said to give to sufferers of arthritis. (It is available from Nichols Garden Nursery; see Sources.)

Calamus *(Araceae)*
It is said that mosquitoes are never found in swamps or other standing water in which calamus, sometimes called sweet flag or sweet root, is growing.

Charlock *(Brassica arvensis)*

Charlock or wild mustard is frequently found in grainfields. The seeds and those of wild radish can lie inert in the ground for 50 to 60 years, showing up again when the field is planted to grain, particularly oats.

Cinquefoil *(Potentilla monspeliensis)*

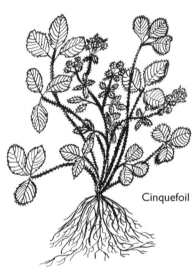

Cinquefoil

The cinquefoils are considered a bad symptom when found on pastureland, for they indicate a very acid soil, and gradually they will choke out other grasses and clovers. They are very persistent and will last when other grasses are burned out by drought. It has been observed that the butternut or gray walnut tree *(Juglans cinerea)* and the black walnut have an inhibitory effect on the growth of the creeping cinquefoil.

Crowfoot (Ranunculaceae)

Like other members of its family, the common meadow buttercup secretes a substance in its roots that poisons the soil for clover by inhibiting the growth of nitrogen bacteria. So potent is this secretion that clover in time will disappear if buttercups begin to invade the field. Cattle will not eat the acrid, caustic plant, and children should be warned against biting the buttercup's stem and leaves, which are capable of raising blisters.

The garden monkshood *(Aconitum)* is even more dangerous, being poisonous in all its parts, while other members of this family that are more or less poisonous are delphinium, columbine, and peony. They are beautiful, but grow them with care.

Cypress Spurge *(Euphorbia cyparissias)*

This funny little plant escaped from eastern gardens where it was grown as an ornamental. The milky juice once was thought to be effective against warts, and it is used in France as a laxative. Here the plant has become a weed. Do not let it grow near grapes, since it may cause the vines to become sterile, and cattle eating hay containing the spurge are made ill.

Dandelion *(Taraxacum officinale)*

Dandelion likes a good, deep soil, as do clover and alfalfa. Soil around dandelions is attractive to earthworms, for this plant is a natural humus producer.

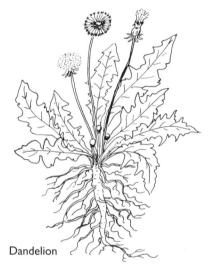

Dandelions on your lawn may frustrate, but actually they are not in competition with the grasses because their three-foot-deep roots take nutrients from a different level of the soil. They penetrate hardpan and bring up minerals, especially calcium, depositing them nearer the surface and thus restoring what the soil has lost by washing. When dandelions die, their root chan-

Dandelion

nels act like an elevator shaft for earthworms, permitting them to penetrate deeper into the soil than they might otherwise.

Dandelions exhale ethylene gas, which limits both the height and growth of neighboring plants. It also causes nearby flowers and fruits to mature early.

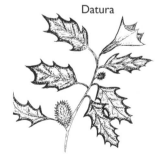

Datura

Datura *(Datura stramonium)*

Other names for this weed are Jamestown weed, jimsonweed, apple of Peru, thorn apple, stink-weed, devil's trumpet, angel's trumpet, and dewtry. Although all parts of datura are poisonous, it is a source of valuable medicine. The weed is especially helpful to pumpkins and it protects other plants from Japanese beetles. The smoke from dried datura leaves is calming to honeybees when opening a hive, but use it sparingly.

Dead Nettle *(Lamium album)*
Although classed as a nettle, this plant, sometimes called white archangel, has no relation to stinging nettle and does not sting. A similarity of the leaves may be the reason for its name. Dead nettle has a long season of showy white bloom and is one of the few herbs that will also grow in damp places in filtered sunlight. As such, it is a valuable companion for the garden and for grain crops.

Devil's Shoestring *(Tephrosia virginiana)*
There are nineteen species of this native North American weed that have valuable insecticidal properties. It is low in toxicity to animals, but is reputed to contain a fish poison. Wild turkeys are fond of eating the plant.

Dock *(Rumex crispus)*
Curled dock is both a food and a medicine. In the old days it was gathered to "thin and purify the blood" in the spring of the year. There is no evidence to support this claim, but the high vitamin C content of dock undoubtedly was beneficial, particularly after a winter diet deficient in greens. The greens also are richer in vitamin A than carrots.

Dock is good to calm the pain of stinging nettle. Crush the juicy leaves and rub on the affected area.

Dyer's Greenweed *(Genista tinctoria)*
Once this was considered a very useful plant for dyeing. Bees like it for its honey and sheep and goats like to graze it, but it is thought that its bitter taste affects the milk of cows that eat it.

Eelgrass *(Zostera marina)*
Eelgrass has an edible grain and is a widely distributed sea plant

along the coasts of North America and Eurasia. It is reportedly harvested in spring by the Seri Indians along the Gulf of California in Sonora, Mexico.

The upper stem fruits in the spring, then breaks off and floats on the surface of the water. The Seri harvest the grain when large quantities of the plant are found floating loose near the shore.

Eelgrass has a content of protein and starch similar to that of grains grown on land. Once it is dry, it is separated from the seaweed with which it grows, and the grains are toasted and ground into flour. Cooked into a gruel, it may be eaten with honey. It is the only ocean plant known that has a grain used as a human food resource.

The Seri find many other uses for the eelgrass, one of which is a cure for diarrhea. It is also piled over house frames for shade and made into toys for the children. Others find it makes an excellent mulch for garden or orchard.

Fresh-water eelgrass (Hydrocharitaceae, genus *Vallisneria*, species *americana),* also known as tapegrass and wild celery, grows in the mud of shallow ponds, sending up ribbonlike leaves directly from the root. (See Sources.)

Euphorbia (Euphorbiaceae)

A few well-placed plants of caper spurge *(Euphorbia lathyrus)* will deter moles and mice and thus are good to plant near young fruit trees. They also are useful to repel rats and mice. Many of the spurge family like dry, light, sandy soils but will spread to cultivated land if given a chance.

Injury to stem or leaves of the euphorbias causes them to exude a milky-looking sap that is very acrid and poisonous. Great care should be taken that the sap does not touch a scratch, as it will even cause blisters on delicate skin. However, the juice of the leafy spurge *(E. elsula)* and the cypress spurge have been used against warts.

Snow-on-the-mountain, one of the euphorbias, is an attractive annual plant that grows wild from Minnesota to Texas. Poinsettia, another lovely member of this family, was formerly considered highly toxic, but is no longer classed as a poisonous plant.

Fern, Male *(Dryopteris filix-mas)*

My beloved old *Pharmacopoeia of the United States of America*, Seventh Decennial Revision, 1890, speaks of this fern eloquently, referring to its taste as "sweetish, acrid, somewhat bitter, astringent and nauseous." It does not, however, say that fern seed will make you invisible, as the Doctrine of Signatures once stated.

That ferns have medicinal value has been recognized for centuries and they are still listed in the *Pharmacopoeia* today, the useful species including also the evergreen wood fern *(D. marginalis)*. In the autumn the roots are carefully dug, cleaned, and dried and the substance oleoresin is extracted through the use of ether.

Perhaps it is because of the oleoresin that ferns and beeches *(Fagus)* have an inhibiting effect on each other. However, a compost made of ferns assists tree seeding and is useful to tree nurseries to encourage germination.

Fiddlehead Fern *(Pteridium aquilinum)*

Sometimes called bracken, fiddlehead fern is another sprout-type wild food. This coarse fern has a single thick base stalking into three distinct curled fronds growing several inches from the ground. This fern is found in low, moist land from Canada southward into Virginia. To gather, snap off the coiled fiddleheads. The coat of fuzz is easily removed by pulling each head through your fingers.

Cook the fiddleheads in boiling water for about an hour, season with pepper, salt, and melted butter, oil and vinegar, or sour cream. Some people like to nibble the fern heads raw. They may also be cooked like asparagus or fresh beans.

Mature fronds may be toxic to grazing animals but as long as the ferns are coiled and tender, we may eat them.

Fleabane *(Erigeron)*

This is one of our native plants that have spread to Europe and taken possession of stony soils. It is used for medicinal purposes, and the acrid oil as a mosquito repellent. But some people are allergic to this plant, reacting to it as they would to poison ivy.

Fungi

Fungi are plants without chlorophyll — some are very useful and even edible, others are very troublesome.

Mushrooms have a natural affinity for plants in woods, fields, and meadows. The part of the mushroom we see is just a small portion of the entire plant. Most of it is underground, a tangled, twisted jungle of threads that form the vegetative part of the plant (mycelium). The mushroom itself is the reproductive part, the fruiting body, which grows easily under the right conditions of moisture and temperature.

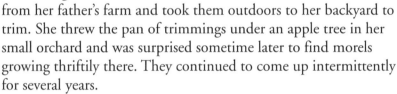

My sister-in-law in Missouri once brought home some morels from her father's farm and took them outdoors to her backyard to trim. She threw the pan of trimmings under an apple tree in her small orchard and was surprised sometime later to find morels growing thriftily there. They continued to come up intermittently for several years.

The delicious morels are fairly common in the United States. The fruit body, like that of other mushrooms, grows above the ground and resembles a sponge. Because of this, they are easy to identify and safe for the collector to gather for the table. They are often found in apple orchards just about the time the trees are blossoming.

Many mushrooms are deadly poison and no one who is inex-

Morchella elata

Morchella semilbera

perienced should ever gather them for food. The deadly amanita, sometimes called the destroying angel, can cause death in less than six hours. Yet many of the poisonous mushrooms also serve a purpose in promoting healthy growth on other plants.

Truffles, another type of fungus, grow several inches below the ground and are not visible. They are rare in the United States but are quite common in Spain, England, Italy, and France, where they grow under oak and chestnut trees. Here they are found by dogs and pigs specially trained to locate them by smell. Should you see a French farmer following a pig on a leash, this is simply a routine way of picking truffles, which sell for fantastic prices.

Because of their close association with oak and chestnut trees, scientists believe that the truffles help the tree roots assimilate chemicals from the soil. Truffles vary from ¼ inch to 4 inches in diameter and resemble an acorn, a walnut, or a potato. The spores are borne within the tuberlike body of the fungus. They have a delicious taste and serve as a condiment. They are black and thus very attractive as a garnish for salads.

Fungus on tree roots first was reported in 1885 by the German botanist A. B. Frank. His belief that water and nutrients were entering the tree through the fungus was scoffed at, but we know today that the fungus acts as a link between the soil and the rootlets of the plant. The tree in turn helps the mycorrhizal fungus by providing root metabolites, substances that are vital to the fungus for the completion of its full life cycle. Harmless tree fungi called saprophytes help trees to resist such diseases as bark canker, decay fungi, and leaf rust fungus.

Mildews are a type of fungi that can be extremely troublesome and difficult to control when they form on plants, usually due to combined moisture and humidity. They attack grapes, lettuce, tomatoes, roses, peas, tobacco, potatoes, cucumbers, and many other fruits and vegetables, usually forming a gray or white, powderlike coating on the surface of the leaves. I have found that it is possible to partly control this fungus with a dusting of wettable sulphur. Sunshine and good air circulation is the best remedy.

Smut is a fungus that attacks such grains as wheat, barley, rye, corn, and oats. It looks like a large sac or tumor among the kernels when it appears on an ear of corn. The sac contains a large mass of black spores.

Smuts act on the host plant in a different way from most parasitic fungi. The mycelium that grows among the cells of the host stimulates them to produce a swelling, or gall. The spores develop as a black mass within the gall and are thrown into the air when the gall breaks.

Smuts are difficult to control as, unlike the spores of any other fungi that attach themselves to the seed, these lie dormant in the ground through the winter. In the spring new kinds of spores are germinated and reinfect the corn plants. Treating the seed is seldom effective in preventing corn smut. The best answer seems to be crop rotation, along with the development and use of strains of corn that are smut-resistant.

Garlic, Meadow *(Allium vineale)*
Meadow garlic's very penetrating taste and odor give a bad taste to milk if eaten by cows, and the bulblets in wheat will spoil the flour. It's hard to eradicate because the little bulbs grow deeper and deeper into the soil with the passing years. If pastures or fields are badly infested, crop rotation is recommended.

But even wild garlic has a definite health value, and medicines derived from it are useful against high blood pressure and sclerosis.

Ginger, Wild Ginger *(Asarum canadensis)*
Ginger grows in rich woods from Virginia to Minnesota on a low plant with root cords extending from a knotty but superficial root. The leathery leaves, mottled green, are heart-shaped, growing on tough, hairy stalks. A reddish brown, cup-shaped flower blooms during April and May at ground level, emerging between two-leaf stalks. Gingerroot is best dug in October when the roots are full and are better for candied ginger at this time.

Ginseng *(Panax quinquefolium)*
Wild ginseng needs the companionship of trees to provide the

filtered sunlight it requires to grow. When raised in beds for commercial use, it is covered with latticework to protect it from the heat of the sun, which would kill it.

The Chinese believe that ginseng will cure nearly every disease, yet even now Western science is not sure whether it has real value or not. Physicians regard its benefits as largely psychological, but tests in Russia and elsewhere indicate that infusions of the root actually may increase energy and resistance to infection.

Goldenrod *(Solidago)*

There are more than 60 native species of goldenrods, some growing on dry soil low in humus, others on soil that is rich and moist. If you would eliminate the goldenrod, cut it before it goes to seed and improve your soil with organic matter and beneficial crops.

Henbane *(Hyoscyamusniger, L.)*

Henbane, like hemp, is an ancient narcotic that was once used to treat disease, but escaped to become naturalized in some parts of the country. The drug hyoscyamine, used to dilate the pupils of the eyes, is made from black henbane.

This poisonous herb is fatal to fowl, hence its name "henbane." All parts of the plant contain poisonous alkaloids, and even hogs sometimes are killed by eating its fleshy roots.

Horsetail *(Equisetum arvense)*

The horsetails are the last remainder of the huge trees of the carboniferous forests. The most common is the field horsetail, which grows in sandy and gravelly soils on a high ground-water level.

Horsetail looks like a tiny Christmas tree and sometimes is called the meadow pine. The hollow-branched, jointed stems range from one to three feet tall. The plant does not produce flowers or seeds but sends up fertile spore-bearing stems resembling catkins. These are covered with powdery brown spores. After the spores drop, small green shoots emerge from the ground. The perennial horsetail has a rootstock that bears tuberous growths that store available carbohydrate against a future need.

The green shoots of horsetail contain a high percentage of silica, the controlling factor against fungus disease. If the green stems are burned in a hot but quiet flame, removing all organic parts, the white skeleton of silica that is left will show the original structure of the little stems.

Silicic acid can be found in many plants such as stinging nettle and quack or couch grass, but some, including horsetail and knotweed *(Polygonum aviculare),* are particularly rich in it. It is this silica in horsetail that has made it valuable medicinally for centuries.

Silicic acid is traditionally believed to strengthen tissue, particularly that of the lungs, and at times to add to disease resistance. It has been reported to have a good influence on inflammation of the

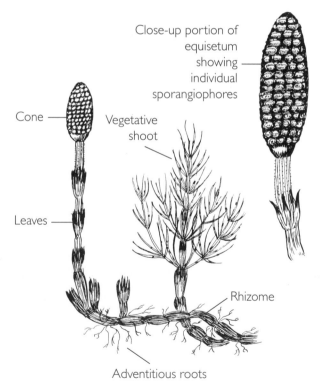

The ancient, primitive horsetail (called equisetum) makes a fine plant spray. The plants, containing much silica, also are used to scour pots and pans.

gums, the mouth, or the skin in general. Horsetail was specially recommended for diuretic purposes by Kneipp, the German priest who
was so successful in using hydrotherapy in combination with herbs.

While horsetail itself will stop external bleeding, a horsetail
brew also may be used as a healing agent for abscesses, burns, cuts,
and scratches, for both animals and humans. Place a good handful
of the dried leaves and stems in a stewpan with just enough
vinegar (5 percent acidity) to cover. Simmer for no longer than 20
minutes, cool, and strain. Keep in the refrigerator. When needed
for use, add 1 part brew to 2 parts cow or goat milk. Return any
not needed to refrigerator. Horsetail brew is stingless, soothing,
and gentle in its action. A plastic squeeze bottle may be used for
convenient application.

A tea made of horsetail is very effective against mildew and
other fungi found on fruit trees, grapevines, vegetables, and roses.
It is gentle but swift in action and does not disturb soil life. Silica-
rich plants are valuable on the compost pile, too.

The parts used are the dried leaves and stems of the sterile
form. Boil 2 or 3 teaspoons of the crumbled herb to a cup of water
for 20 minutes. Or soak the leaves in water for several hours, boil
for 10 minutes, and steep for another 10.

Made into a spray, it is particularly useful against powdery fungus
and curly leaf on peach trees. It also controls mildew on roses, vegetables, grapes, and stone fruits, and has been found to have a cell-
strengthening action on the plants sprayed with it.

According to Beatrice Trum Hunter's *Gardening Without
Poisons*, silica in the form of an aerogel is one of our most effective
insecticides. It may be used against the flour beetle, rice weevil,
granary weevil, and the larva of the Mediterranean flour moth.

Horsetails have still another use: Their high silica content
makes them effective as "scouring brushes" for pots and pans,
and campers still find them usually available and convenient for
this purpose. In German-speaking countries horsetail was called
Zinnkraut, or "pewter plant," because the high silica content made
it useful for cleaning and scrubbing copper, brass, pewter, and all
fine metals.

Indian Cucumber *(Medeola virginiana)*

Indian cucumbers are found from the Great Lakes eastward and south to Florida in rich woodlands. They are good eaten raw, cubed in salad, or pickled. "They grow in sociable groups," says Grace Firth in *A Natural Year*, "and, like other sociables, are best when mildly pickled."

The single slender stems of Indian cucumbers grow out of a whorl of five or seven dark, elongate, visibly ribbed leaves. The spindly cream-colored flowers are followed by small black berries. The roots grow horizontally just below the ground surface, making the cucumbers easy to dig.

Jewelweed *(Impatiens bifora* or *I. pallida)*

Jewelweed is an excellent remedy for poison ivy, relieving the itching almost instantly. It does not have an adverse effect on the poison ivy plants, for the two often grow side by side. In fact, wherever poison ivy grows, jewelweed is likely in the vicinity. It blooms between July and September.

Jewelweed

To make the remedy, boil a potful of jewelweed in water until the liquid is about half the original volume. The strained juice is effective both in preventing the rash after exposure and in treating the rash after it has developed. The best way to keep the extract is frozen and stored in cubes in the freezer. Pack them in small plastic bags and they will be at hand if needed.

The young, tender sprouts of jewelweed are edible and are cooked like green beans.

Knotweed *(Polygonum aviculare)*

These members of the Buckwheat family grow mostly on acid soils. The prostrate knotweed, frequently found in garden borders and along paths, doesn't mind being trampled on. All knotweeds are characterized by "knots" on their stems from which branches grow.

Knotweeds in pastures are thought to be troublesome to sheep. They also inhibit the growth of turnips, and are very rich in silica.

Lamb's-Quarters *(Chenopodium album)*
This plant, sometimes called smooth pigweed, is one of our most enduring annual weeds, producing a tremendous amount of seeds that are able to survive dormant in the soil for decades. It is among the weeds that follow human footsteps and cultivation, liking a soil with a well-fermented humus.

Lamb's-quarters is particularly stimulated when grown with potatoes, and it should be allowed to grow in the garden in moderate amounts, especially with corn. It also aids cucumber, muskmelon, pumpkin, and watermelon as well as giving additional vigor to zinnias, marigolds, peonies, and pansies.

This plant, a close relative of spinach, also is good to eat. The young shoots may be cooked and eaten like asparagus. It is richer in vitamin C than spinach, far richer in vitamin A, and, though not quite so rich in iron and potassium, is still a good source of these minerals. It is exceptionally rich in calcium.

Lamb's-quarters is a freebie that everyone should know about, for it is found in cultivated ground from north to south and east to west, and plants in the right stage for eating can usually be found from late spring until frost. It even grows in the Andes at a height of 12,000 feet, and here has become an important substitute for rye and barley, which cannot survive at such an altitude.

Larkspur, Wild (Ranunculaceae)
Wild larkspur is detrimental to cattle and too much may cause poisoning. Barley as a crop, however, is a weed deterrent and will prevent wild larkspur or poppy from establishing itself. It is thought to promote vigor in winter wheat.

Locoweed *(Astragalus mollissimus* and *A. diphysus)*
Locoweed gets its name from the Spanish word for crazy, due to the strange actions of animals poisoned by it.

Strangely enough, the poisonous effect of locoweed depends

on the soil in which the plants grow, because of their ability to absorb poisonous elements from the soil. Both the green and the dry plants are poisonous, the symptoms varying somewhat in horses, cattle, and sheep.

Horses become dull, drag their legs, seldom eat, lose muscle control, become thin, and then die. Cattle react similarly, but sometimes they run about wildly, or stagger and bump into objects in their path. Sheep are less apt to be injured by the poison.

Ranchers destroy locoweed by cutting the roots about two inches below the surface.

Lupine *(Lupinus perennis)*

Sometimes called old maid's bonnets, wild pea, or sundial, the plant has vivid blue flowers, sometimes pink or white, with a butterfly shape that indicates its membership in the Legume family.

Farmers once thought that lupines preyed upon the fertility of their soil; hence the name derived from *lupus,* "a wolf." In fact, they help the growth of corn, as well as most other cultivated crops.

Lupines grow best on steep, gravelly banks or exposed sunny hills, liking almost worthless land where their roots can penetrate to surprising depths, in time leaving behind them fine, friable soil. They are adventurous pioneers, spreading far and wide in thrifty colonies, and are among the first plants to grow on the barren pumice after a volcanic eruption.

The lupine is one of those interesting flowers that go to sleep at night. Some fold their leaflets not only at night but also during the day when there is movement in the leaves. Sundial, a popular name for the wild lupine, refers to this peculiarity. Among the nearly 100 kinds of lupines that grow in North America, some contain poisonous alkaloids, while the seeds of others can be eaten.

Mayweed *(Anthemis cotula)*

Sometimes this is called dog fennel or fetid camomile because of its evil smell. Beekeepers used to rub it into their skin to repel bees. It also will repel fleas and may be rubbed into floors and walls of a granary to repel mice.

Meadow Pink *(Lychnis floscuculi)*

The roots of all members of the Lychnis family contain saponin, which produces a soapy foam if stirred in water. Before the invention of soap these roots, together with those of the true saponaria, were used for washing. An interesting family member is the sleepy catchfly, so called because its flowers are closed most of the day, opening only in bright sunshine, while the gluey substance on its stems entangles flies.

Mildew, Powdery (Erysiphaceae)

Mildew is a fungus of the type called an "obligate parasite" because it feeds on living plants. When moisture conditions are just right, wind-carried spore (little seeds) resting on a plant's leaves send out germ tubes, which grow into white threads (mycelia). These branch over the leaves in a white, soft, felty coating.

This type of fungus does not grow *inside* the plant but sends its little suckers (haustoria) into the plant's sap. As chains are built up from the mycelium spore, the plant becomes covered in a few days. Eventually black fruiting bodies with the sexual or "overwintering" spores are formed.

Because it is on the surface, mildew is more easily controlled than many other fungi, and horsetail tea is an excellent spray to use (see *Horsetail* in this chapter). During the season when green plants are available, it is also good to prepare an extract by covering freshly picked plants with water. Allow them to ferment for about 10 days, then dilute the liquid and use it as a spray in the same way as the tea. Mustard seed flour or sulphur dust also may be used, while polybutenes, oil derivatives, have been used successfully to control powdery mildew on cucurbits.

Milkweed *(Asclepias)*

All of the many milkweeds exude milky juice when their leaves or stems are punctured. Roots are considered poisonous, but Native Americans have used them for various maladies, and some say that the juice cures warts or ringworm. Cows dislike the bitter, acrid plants but may eat them if hard-pressed for food.

Mistletoe (Loranthaceae)

This parasite is the most legendary of plants. It was sacred to the ancient Druids, who cut it with a golden sickle (the symbol of the sun) and caught it in a cloth to prevent it from touching the ground.

Mistletoe grows on apple trees, oaks, and poplars, usually being sown by birds. Here in Oklahoma it is our state "flower" and grows profusely on hackberry trees.

People used to call the mistletoe "all heal" and thought there was no illness it could not cure. It is in fact poisonous, particularly the berries. If you find it growing on your trees, remove it, for it is a parasite and eventually will weaken the tree and possibly kill it.

Nettles

See *Stinging Nettle*.

Nightshade (Solanaceae)

The Nightshade family includes apple-of-Sodom, belladonna, bittersweet, capiscum, eggplant, jimsonweed *(datura)*, petunia, potato, snakeberry, tobacco, and tomato.

Where black nightshade *(Solanum nigrum)* grows profusely, the soil is tired of growing root crops. This plant draws the Colorado potato beetle away from potatoes, since they prefer the weed though it is poisonous. The beetles eat it and die.

Nut Grass *(Cyperus esculentus)*

The botanical name, *Cyperus esculentus,* means "edible sedge." Nut grass is related to the tules and bulrushes and is almost as old as civilization. The ancient Egyptians developed cultivated strains more than five thousand years ago. The "nut", which is really a tuber, may be made into many tasty and unusual dishes. But consider well before growing this plant, for it can become a fearful weed. Having battled against it in my garden for many years, I have come to the conclusion that this is a plant only Euell Gibbons could love.

If the native species of nut grass plagues you, it can be discouraged by growing a heavy cover crop of cowpeas on the plot for several summers. Sow the cowpeas thickly to form a dense mat that shades the ground. Plow them under in late fall, in October or November, and they will add nitrogen to the soil. St. Augustine grass will choke out nut grass on a lawn.

Opuntia (Cactaceae)

In the Southwest and Mexico, people eat the flat-leaved joints on opuntia cactus boiled or fried, and make the flowers into salads. The juicy fruits of opuntia are eaten raw or cooked; the seeds are ground up into a meal and made into cakes. The bushy cacti grow in hedges around houses, and where little else will survive they serve as windbreaks and ground cover.

In some regions in times of drought ranchers "burn off" the cactus spines so that cattle may eat the plants. Plant breeder Luther Burbank developed a spineless cactus that proved to be a useful source of food for both men and animals, and in some sections of California the opuntia type is a commercial crop. It is grown on sandy loam, fertilized with chicken manure, and needs no insecticides. The crop of young leaves, which measure about eight inches long at one to two months, are hand-picked to be sold diced, shredded, and spiced, or pickled.

Opuntia

Almost all of the many useful species of cactus will grow well with each other, requiring the same type of soil and cultural practices. Many have beautiful delicate blossoms and are grown as ornamentals, and there is a subzero cactus of the opuntia type that will grow in the North. (See Sources.)

Ox-eye Daisy *(Chrysanthemum leucanthemum)*

Ox-eye daisy seeds are beneficial in small quantity mixed (1 to 100) with wheat grains, but in larger quantity the daisy will overwhelm the wheat.

Pansy, Wild *(Viola tricolor)*

The wild form of the cultivated pansy is Shakespeare's "heartsease," and once was listed in the *U.S. Pharmacopoeia* as a medicine. Many species of viola were candied as a sweet and were thought to be soothing and therapeutic to the heart.

Rye helps the wild pansy to germinate and is itself seemingly improved by a few pansies. But the pansy has an inhibiting effect on wheat.

Pawpaw Trees *(Asimina triloba)*

These quick-growing, rangy trees rarely exceed 20 feet but bear large, outsized leaves. The fruit usually falls to the ground before it is good to eat but will ripen if held at room temperature. Mashed pawpaws may be made into a bread similar to banana bread.

Pennycress *(Thlaspi arvens)*

Like shepherd's purse, this is often abundant where grain is grown. The seeds are 20 percent oil, and if accidentally ground with grain will spoil the flour. Mountain pennycress *(Thlaspi alpestre* var. *calaminare)* likes soils containing zinc.

Peruvian Ground Cherry *(Nicandra physalodes)*

When planted in quantity near a barn or in a stableyard it will repel flies, and it also is effective against whitefly.

Pigweed

See *Amaranth* in this chapter.

Plantain *(Plantago)*

Plantain

Of the many different plantain species, the large-bracted plantain *(P. aristata)* is the most prolific, one plant producing well over 3,000 seeds.

The narrow-leaved *(P. lanceolata)* has been used as a home remedy for treating bruises and strained joints. It also has a cooling and astringent effect if a few leaves are squeezed over a bee sting.

Plantain and red clover frequently are found growing together, this because the plantains occur as impurities in grass and clover seeds. If plantains appear on the lawn, it is best to dig them out.

Poison Ivy *(Rhus radicans)*

Poison ivy

Jewelweed will relieve the itching of poison ivy (see *Jewelweed*). If your land has poison ivy, the best thing you can do is eradicate it. Mow close to the ground in midsummer and follow this with plowing and harrowing, grubbing out small patches. Under trees or along a fence where mowing might be difficult, try smothering it with heavy cardboard or tar paper. A deep mulch of hay or straw may work as well.

Vines growing in trees may be cut near the ground and then pulled down a few days later. Be sure to wear gloves and protective clothing, washing well afterward, preferably with yellow soap.

Pokeweed *(Phytolacca americana)*

I find that pokeweed grows well under my figs, Scotch pines, and other trees. Pokeberries and roots are poisonous, but the tiny, pinkish green, asparagus-like shoots are simply delicious. Poke is one of the first greens to come up in early spring, and these shoots should be cooked lightly in several changes of water. The berries and roots contain phytolaccin, a cathartic and slightly narcotic substance used for treating rheumatism.

Pokeweed

Poke should never be confused with the completely unrelated Indian poke, or white hellebore. This latter plant, also poisonous, grows in wet places and comes up very early in the spring before the edible poke starts growing.

Potherbs

There is a wealth of wild greens available in April. Most of these belong to the Mustard family, Cruciferae, so called because their flower petals form a cross. The mustard cousins, Brassica, together with strong-growing young shoots of peppergrass *(Lepidium)*, horseradish *(Armoracia lapathifolia)*, pennycress *(Thlaspi arvens)*, searocket *(Cakile edentula)*, scurvy grass *(Cochlearia)*, and other cress greens are a gift of spring to those who love to search for wild greens. Cook them as you would turnip greens or spinach. If their turnipy-horseradishy flavor is a bit much for you, combine them with milder greens such as young amaranth *(Amaranthus)*, Japanese knotweed *(Polygonum cuspidatum)*, or dayflowers *(Commelina communis)*. Shepherd's purse *(Capsella bursa-pastoris)* also combines well. Gather potherbs when the shoots are very young. You may wish to cook them through several waters.

Puffball (Fungi)

Sometimes these "smoke balls" or "devil's snuffboxes" grow to be more than two feet across. A cut that is bleeding profusely may be covered with the powderlike spores from those that produce a puff or "smoke" when disturbed, and it will stop the bleeding. Puffball powder is very explosive, so if you store it, keep the container closed and away from fire.

Purslane *(Portulaca oleracea)*

Purslane has a liking for good cultivated soil and is frequently found in gardens. But it is not altogether unwelcome, for though often considered a weed, it is cultivated in both England and Holland. It is a refreshing green with a slightly acid taste, and it may be cooked like spinach. One hundred grams of purslane contains 3.5 milligrams of iron, and this is all the more remarkable because the plant is 92.5 percent water.

Pyrethrum *(Chrysanthemum cinerariaefolium)*
Pyrethrum is absolutely bugproof and will keep pests from plants
close by. Few ticks are ever found where pyrethrum or sage forms a
ground cover. Pyrethrum powder, generally considered a safe insecticide, is made from the dried flowers. It has a very short residual
action, breaking down rapidly in sunlight. Because of this it can be
used as a preharvest spray.

Records show that pyrethrum may have been used nearly two
thousand years ago in China. As an insect repellent it became popular again in the nineteenth century, when it was the "secret ingredient" in Persian insect powder. In 1828 this powder was produced
on a commercial scale and introduced into Europe by an
Armenian trader. By 1860 it was becoming well known in the
United States.

The active principles in pyrethrum are the esters pyrethrin and
cinerin. Certain nontoxic plant products such as asarinin (from the
bark of southern prickly ash), sesamin (from sesame oil), and
peperine (from black pepper) are added to pyrethrum to
strengthen its effect.

Rattlebox *(Crotalaria)*
This weed is valuable for its soil-improving qualities, but one
variety, *C. sagittalis,* found on bottomland in the Missouri and
Mississippi basin, is very poisonous to cattle and horses and should
be eradicated. Following its cutting or plowing under, plant a crop
like cotton or corn that needs repeated cultivation.

St.-John's-Wort *(Hypericum perforatum)*
This common pasture plant contains a red oil sometimes used as a
home remedy for bronchitis and chest colds. It also is astringent
and has been used against diarrhea and dysentery. The leaves have
oily cells and a strong, peculiar smell. They look perforated if held
against the light. It was once believed that if the plant was collected during St. John's Night (June 24), it would afford protection
against witches and evil spirits.

Shepherd's Purse *(Capsella bursa-pastoris)*

Shepherd's purse is very rich in minerals. Along with mustard, it absorbs excessive salts in the soil and returns them in organic form. If grown on a salty marsh and plowed under while still green, it will both sweeten the soil and discourage the weeds ordinarily growing on such soil. It has medicinal qualities and has been used as a styptic.

Sow Thistle *(Sonchus arvensis)*

This plant has creeping, deep-growing roots, contains a milky, yellow-tinged juice, and grows on moist soil. It aids watermelon, muskmelon, pumpkin, and cucumber and in moderate amounts onions, tomatoes, and corn.

A cousin called blessed thistle *(Cnicus benedictus)* has medicinal and industrial uses and is a basic ingredient of the Benedictine liqueur as well as certain bitter tonics.

Spurge

See *Euphorbia* in this chapter.

Stinging Nettle *(Urtica dioica)*

Stinging nettle has many helpful qualities. It makes neighboring plants more insect-resistant. It also helps plants withstand lice, slugs, and snails during wet weather; strengthens growth of mint and tomatoes; and gives greater aromatic quality to herbs such as valerian, angelica, marjoram, sage, and peppermint. The nettle protects fruit from mold and thus enables it to keep better. Fruit packed in nettle hay ripens more quickly.

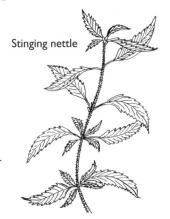

Stinging nettle

Stinging nettle is helpful to stimulate fermentation in compost or manure piles, according to British author M. E. Bruce, who advises making a crushed nettle solution. Good results can be had with less trouble by using the nettle in its original form, placing it in layers in the compost before the nettle seeds ripen. The plant is said to contain carbonic acid and ammonia, and these may be the factors that activate the compost. If you have the space, you might try raising a crop of nettle — somewhere away from the garden, for the plant spreads quickly.

Euell Gibbons reports that stinging nettles combined with young horseradish leaves are delicious as spring greens. They also combine well with lettuce or spinach. Since nettles are rich in vitamins and iron, they are a good remedy for anemia, while aiding blood circulation and acting as a stimulant.

The plant leaves, as rich in protein as cottonseed meal, are good for animals, too, though they will touch them only when the nettles are mowed and dried. Horses improve in health and cows will give more and richer milk. When powdered nettle leaves are added to their mash, hens will lay more eggs and the eggs will have a higher food value, chicks will grow faster, and turkeys will fatten. Even the manure from nettle-fed animals is better than that from others.

Be sure to wear gloves when picking young nettles, for the fine hairs on the leaves and stems contain formic acid, which irritates the skin when touched. Nettle rash can be relieved with the juice of the nettle plant itself, or by rubbing the skin with jewelweed, with rhubarb, or with any member of the Sorrel family.

Tansy *(Tanacetum vulgare)*

Tansy, once used as a medicinal tea, is now considered dangerous if taken as an infusion (see the chapter on Poisonous Plants). It is also thought to be poisonous to cattle. But planted under fruit trees, particularly peach, it repels borers, and is a good companion to roses, raspberries, blackberries, grapes, and other cane fruits. It deters flying insects, Japanese beetles, striped cucumber beetles, and squash bugs, and helps repel flies and ants. The dried leaves are useful for

Tansy

storing woolens and furs. Because of its concentration of potassium, tansy is useful on the compost pile.

Tansy also goes by the names of bitter buttons, ginger plant, hind heal, and scented fern. Its fernlike, attractive foliage is topped by composite heads of buttonlike flowers, and their scent is delightful. Though the roots have been used, it is the tops that are of primary importance.

Tansy once was used as a culinary herb in place of pepper, was widely used in churches in medieval times as a "strewing herb," and is one of the plants associated with the Virgin Mary.

Thistle *(Circium)*

All thistles are rich in potassium and thus are useful in compost; but their prickly leaves make them unpopular in pasture, and certain types rob grainfields of food and moisture. To kill out thistles, be careful not to cut them before the blossoms are open or many more will grow from the rootstocks. If you cut just the blossom heads after the blossoms are pollinated, the plant will bleed to death.

Blessed thistle *(Cnicus benedictus)* has medicinal and industrial uses, as well as being an insect repellent, while constituting a basic ingredient of the Benedictine liqueur and stomach bitters.

Thornapple *(Datura stramonium)*

See *Datura* in this chapter.

Tillandsia *(T. usneoides)*

Tillandsia (also called Spanish moss, though not a true moss) occurs naturally from Virginia to Florida and Texas and southward to Argentina and Chile. Though it may be seen on other trees, its favorite host is the live oak. It is not a parasite, sapping the life of the tree, but a lodger that finds its own food supply through slender, grayish stems that look like hair hanging from the trees. It is related to the air plants of the Bromelia or Pineapple family, which largely draw their sustenance from the air itself. It may be used for mulching or for compost. The dried stems also are used industrially to stuff upholstery.

Venus Flytrap *(Dionaea muscipula)*

This hungry little plant, which captures its own meals, must be grown in high humidity indoors or out. The insect traps on young plants, which develop in three to four weeks, consist of two leaves hinged in the center when open, and when closed forming a pouch in which the trapped insects are digested. When a leaf has caught several insects it withers and dies, but new ones take its place. Venus flytrap grows naturally in bogs where the soil lacks available nitrogen, and the insects supply this nutrient in the plant's diet.

Water Hyacinth *(Eichhornia crassipes)*

This tropical American plant has "escaped" and is now growing profusely in the southern states, sometimes choking ponds and streams with its growth of floating leaves. The roots hang down in the water and receive the spawn of fish. The lovely violet flowers are large and showy.

If you live in an area where water hyacinth has gone wild, you will benefit both yourself and the waterway by dredging it out and using it for compost.

Water Lily *(Nymphaea odorata)*

The American water lily, related to the lotus, sends long, stout leaf and flower stalks from the mud bottom of clear, shallow water. The beautiful flowers usually rise above the water on long stalks and may be as large as a foot across. In cultivation, water lilies grow well in a mixed planting of other water plants. In the wild state they, like water hyacinth, sometimes threaten to choke shallow pools of water and should be dredged out and composted.

Weeds

Someone once said, "A weed is a plant out of place," but I am inclined to go along with Ralph Waldo Emerson, who believed that "a weed is a plant whose virtues have not yet been discovered." Weeds, wisely used, are some of our most important companion plants. Of course, they never should be allowed to overwhelm the food plants, but a few left here and there may surprise you by the influence they exert.

The extensive root growth of weeds penetrates the subsoil, breaking it up and making it easier for the roots of crop plants to go farther than usual as they search for water and nourishment. A few weeds are useful in shading the ground to keep seedling vegetables from drying out in the sun's heat. Meanwhile, moisture from the subsoil will travel by capillary action up the outside of the weed roots to a level where the young vegetables can use it.

Deep divers such as pigweed, lamb's-quarters, and thistles bring up minerals from the lower soil by way of their stalks and leaves. When these weeds are turned under, the minerals become available to shallower-rooting crops. Minerals, including trace minerals that may be leached away or become exhausted under a succession of crops, are thus retained.

Another interesting fact is that weeds seem to accumulate the nutrients in which a particular soil is deficient. Such weeds as sheep sorrel and plantain, which thrive best in acid soil, are rich in alkalinizing minerals such as calcium and magnesium. Bracken, which grows best in phosphorus-poor soil, is high in phosphorus. Turning these weeds under will release these minerals into the topsoil, again making them available to food plants.

Weeds also benefit the soil by conditioning it. Their extensive root sytems leave fibrous organic matter, which decays, adding humus to both topsoil and subsoil. Not only this, but they also leave channels for drainage and aeration. When decomposed, the root systems of dandelions provide subterranean channels for earthworms, which, in turn, enrich the soil with their castings. Soil texture is vastly improved and soil-inhabiting bacteria will multiply enormously.

Learning to read weeds can be very useful, for they are excellent indicators of the type of soil they select to grow on.

Weeds that delight in acid soil, and also indicate increasing acidity, are the docks, fingerleaf weeds, lady's thumb, and sorrels. Horsetail indicates slightly acid soil, as do hawkweed and knapweed.

Weeds that indicate a crust formation and hardpan are pennycress, morning glory, horse nettle, field mustard, camomiles, quack grass, and pineapple weed.

Weeds most likely to occur on cultivated land are chickweed, buttercup, dandelion, lamb's-quarters, plantain, nettle, prostrate knotweed, prickly lettuce, field speedwell, common horehound, celandine, mallows, rough pigweed, and carpetweed.

Sandy soils are favored by arrow-leaved wild lettuce, yellow toadflax, onions, partridge pea, broom bush, flowered aster, and most goldenrods.

On alkaline soils we are apt to find sagebrush and woody aster, while limestone soils grow field peppergrass, hare's ear mustard, wormseed, Canada bluegrass, cornelian cherry, pennycress, Barnaby's thistle, mountain bluet, yellow camomile, and field madder.

If a plot of land grows healthy weeds, it will probably grow good vegetable crops, too. Let the weeds reach full growth but cut them before they go to seed. Let them wilt a few days and then plow them under for green manure.

You may even find it helpful to your compost pile to bring in extra weeds such as those cut by the highway department along public roadways. This largesse often includes such items as nettles, sunflowers, yarrows, and sweet clover. These should be thoroughly composted to kill their seeds before being placed on the garden.

Weeds are not necessarily our enemies. With good management, they may well become friends and coworkers.

Wild Carrot *(Daucus carota)*

Wild carrot does not always indicate bad soil, for its deep taproot implies a deep soil capable of good cultivation. A rich stand indicates a soil worth improving for crops. But it can become a pest, so prevent it from seeding by cutting the plant close to the ground shortly after pollination. Do not cut too early or many plants will spread out from the root.

Wild Morning Glory (Convolvulaceae)

We have it from Native Americans that wild morning glory is ben-

Wild morning glory

eficial to corn, but if allowed to go to seed it can become a great pest, coming up for years afterward. It may be killed out by spraying a little white vinegar into the center of each vine.

Wild Parsnip *(Pastinaca sativa)*
Wild parsnip is a nourishing food plant that will give a good yield even on poor soils, but it soon becomes a weed and is hard to eradicate. The cow parsnip *(Heracleum lanatum)* is poisonous.

Wild Radish *(Paphanus raphanistrum)*
Wild radish spreads quickly in soils worn out from growing too many grain crops and depleted in nitrogen. It flourishes well, especially in wet years, where manure is scarce and potassium fertilizer abundant. Nevertheless, cattle are very fond of it, and it produces a good honey as well as an oil from the seed.

Wild Rose (Eglantine)
When this pretty weed migrates from hedgerows to pastures, it indicates the pasture has not been grazed adequately and needs mowing and harrowing. The prickly canes are troublesome to sheep and cattle but do not particularly bother goats, which love all kinds of rosebushes. To eradicate, cut the canes while they are still soft.

Wild Strawberry *(Fragaria)*
Wild strawberries are small, but have a delicious flavor quite unlike any other. Their presence in pastureland is an indicator of increasing acidity.

Yarrow *(Achillea millefolium)*
Yarrow is a plant of both mystery and history. For centuries the

Chinese mystic has cast yarrow stalks
when consulting the *I Ching.*

According to the Bio-Dynamic
book *Companion Plants,* yarrow has a
definite effect on the quality of neighboring plants, increasing not so much
their size as their resistance to adverse
conditions, and thereby improving
their health. It is a good companion
for medicinal herbs, enhancing their
essential oils and increasing their
vitality. It is also said to help cuts to
heal.

Yarrow

Yarrow also gives nearby plants resistance to insects, perhaps
because of its acrid, bitterly pungent odor.

Yarrow tea or yarrow hay is helpful to sheep, and I have given
it to milk goats after kidding. It will grow almost anywhere and
under any conditions and does not mind being walked upon.
Where it grows in lawns and is cut by the mower, it simply spreads
out in a low growth.

Grasses, Grains, and Field Crops

Sugarcane and bamboo are both giant grasses, while the great cereals of the world, grasses too, are wheat, corn, oats, rye, barley, and rice. Wild grasses include bluegrass, esparto, reed, sandbur, Sudan grass, and wild barley, as well as many others.

Many grains and grasses grow well planted together, the growth of both being enhanced and increased.

Cotton *(Gossypium)*

Alfalfa planted before cotton will put nitrogen in the soil, to the cotton's benefit, and alfalfa planted with it will discourage root rot.

Cotton growers try to keep the pink bollworm under control by isolating infected fields, sterilizing seeds and cotton, and by using machines that chop up leaves and other trash from the cotton. Shredding stalks in late summer and plowing them under helps control the worm and the boll weevil.

Farmers now protect their crops against the diseases of older cotton plants by growing varieties that are bred to resist such diseases as wilt and blight.

Crabgrass *(Digitaria sanguinalis)*

Crabgrass is one of the most troublesome lawn pests. Hand-pulling is recommended on lawns (before the plants form a mat), and mulch and frequent cultivation in gardens. As with Bermuda grass, dry hot weather will wilt the roots if they are brought to the surface. (See also *Grass, Quack.*)

Esparsette *(Onobrychis viciaefolia)*

This perennial forage legume of Eurasian origin also is called medick, sanfoin, lucifer, snail clover, and great trefoil. The plant was introduced into England by the Romans, but it is not much grown today, possibly because it takes several years to reach fruition. It produces three crops a year, however, and grows again from the same roots once it reaches maturity. Oddly enough, in England the spikelike flowers are violet but in China they are yellow.

Esparsette is a good food for cattle and is equally nourishing for humans. It is valuable for those suffering from weight loss yet reduces weight in those who are too heavy. It is considered a tonic for both the brain and spinal cord. The roots of a variety called black medick make a good tooth powder.

Esparsette is recommended as a border plant for small grains or vegetables, and in a thin stand it aids growth of corn. It also may be grown as a lightly scattered stand with small grains. The seed retains viability for up to three years, and grows well in limestone soils.

Flax *(Linum usitatissimum)*

Flax is a good companion to both carrots and potatoes, improving both their growth and flavor. Flax planted near potatoes will protect against the Colorado potato beetle. (It is, however, poisonous; see the chapter on Poisonous Plants.)

Leaf extracts of the false flax *(Camelina sativa* and *C. microcarpa),* frequently found growing in flax fields, have an inhibiting effect on flax itself.

Grass, Korean *(Zoysia japonica)*
This group of eastern Asiatic, perennial creeping grasses is widely used in the Southwest. Some are important horticulturally as lawn grasses, others as ornamentals. In hot, dry climates Korean grass is strikingly effective planted with such succulents as the porcelain-like aeonium, the texture contrast enhancing both plants. It grows well with *Cotyledon undulata* and the delicately beautiful rosettes of *Graptopetalum paraguayense*.

Grass, Molasses *(Mellimus minutiflora)*
See *Molasses Grass* in the Pest Control chapter.

Grass, Pampas *(Cortaderia)*
This ornamental grass, best grown in the South, produces beautiful flower plumes that, if cut when fully developed, are useful for decorative purposes indoors during the winter. It is increased by root division, and it grows well as a specimen plant in the lawn.

Grass, Quack *(Agropyron repens* or *Triticum repens)*
Quack grass indicates a crust formation and/or a hardpan in the soil. Choke it out by sowing millet, soybeans, or cowpeas, making sure that the land first is thoroughly cultivated and the weather hot and dry. Two successive crops of rye also will choke it out.

A concentrated brine of common salt (sodium chloride) will kill it out, too, if used after grass is freshly cut and applied in dry weather several times. Dry weather will wilt the roots of quack grass if they are brought to the surface. Hand-pulling is recommended if there are but a few plants.

Like so many other things, quack grass isn't all bad. It is a good cattle feed, and because of its persistence it makes a useful covering for gullies and road banks where live soil has been cut open and few other plants will grow. Though hard to get rid of once it is started, it does prepare the soil for better things. Oddly, it is wheat's nearest relative.

Grasses, Lawn

Bermuda Grass (Cynodon dactylon) is an excellent lawn grass for the southern states. Bermuda withstands both heat and drought and will grow reasonably well even on poor soils. It may be started by seeding or sodding.

Never allow Bermuda to get started in the garden or flower beds, for it spreads quickly on cultivated soil, competing with flowers or vegetables for moisture. It may be killed out in the summer by hoeing and exposing the rhizomes to hot sunlight.

Kentucky Bluegrass (Poa) is an excellent grass for the North and East. It needs a quick-germinating and quick-growing grass, such as redtop, planted with it to provide a rapid ground cover that will help crowd out weeds during its early development. After it gets a good start,the bluegrass will crowd out the nurse grass.

St. Augustine (Stenotaphrum secundatum) also thrives in the South, being particularly good under trees or in other shady areas where Bermuda will not do well. It forms a thick mat and smothers weeds.

Zoysia (Gramineae spp.) in cultivated species forms dense turf and is very valuable for planting on sandy soils, especially in the South. It is propagated vegetatively by means of small pieces of turf called plugs. Zoysia will choke out crabgrass and weeds.

Grasses, Pasture

With the development of "beefalo" hybrid cattle by D. C. Basolo of Tracy, California, rich pasture grasses suitable for grazing livestock take on even greater importance. The Beefalo, which is three-eighths buffalo, three-eighths Charolais, and one-quarter Hereford, can be produced more economically than other breeds because it gains weight faster and can finish out on grass rather than grain.

Another oldtime breed is the Texas Longhorn, which, though not as tasty as the Beefalo, also will finish out on grass.

Bermuda (Cynodon dactylon), a very persistent and nutritious grass of the southern United States, is useful for both pasture and lawn.

Buffalo grass (Buchloe dactyloides), which grows on the western range where bison used to graze, still serves as food for herds of cattle. It is also useful for binding the soil, preventing erosion.

Grama grass (Bouteloua spp.), occurring mostly in the Great Plains area, is excellent forage for livestock. It is widely used also in conservation to prevent soil erosion.

Johnson grass (Sorghum halepense) grows wild all over the Southwest and is often a great pest in gardens, yet in pastures it is very nutritious for cattle.

Ryegrass (Lolium spp.) is often grown in nut orchards and serves as food for cattle that are allowed to graze and fertilize the land, from which they are removed at harvest time. Orchard grass growing under fruit trees can suppress the root growth of pears and apples.

Teosinte (Zea mexicana), an annual grass often used as fodder for livestock, is considered the nearest relative to maize or Indian corn of all the wild grasses. It grows wild in moist soil from Connecticut west to Kansas and south to Florida and Texas.

Nurse Grass

A quick-germinating and quick-growing grass such as redtop frequently is used in lawn seed mixtures to provide a rapid ground cover that helps to crowd out weeds during the early development of the more permanent grasses, such as Kentucky bluegrass. The bluegrass may take two or three years to reach full development, but once it attains this under favorable conditions, it will crowd out the nurse grass.

Oats *(Avena sativa)*

A cover crop of mixed clover and oats following sod and before corn is planted will lessen the white grubs that infest corn. Oats and vetch do well planted together.

Oats sometimes can be grown effectively as a trap crop to lure red-winged blackbirds away from other grains. The stand should be grown at some distance from the birds' roosting places.

Pasture Weeds

Do not let sneezeweed *(Helenium autumnale)*, sometimes called swamp sunflower, grow in pastures. Most cows respect the bitter leaves, but many a pail of milk has been spoiled by a mouthful of helenium among the herbage. If you are wondering why this plant is called sneezeweed, take a whiff of snuff made from the dried and powdered leaves.

Wild larkspur is poisonous to cattle.

Other plants that should never be allowed to grow in pastures are the field and the meadow garlic *(Allium vineale resp. canadense)*. Just a few minutes after a cow has eaten some field garlic her entire body is penetrated, and after half an hour the milk is flavored with it and remains so for several hours. To avoid damage to the milk, it may be necessary to keep the cows off the pasture or let them graze for only a short time after milking, then remove them to another pasture.

Poppy *(Papaver* spp.)

Poppy and wild larkspur like to grow with winter wheat but dislike barley. Wheat fields heavily infested with poppy yield a poor harvest of lightweight seeds.

Poppies are grown for both seed and oil but they rob the soil of nutrients, causing it to need rest and reinforcement afterward. This factor may be used to advantage, however, to choke out weeds that cannot be gotten rid of by any other means.

Poppy seeds may lie dormant in the ground for years and then show up again with a grain crop, particularly winter wheat.

Poppies can become too much of a good thing, especially in plantings of barley, which they inhibit.

Rape *(Brassica napus)*

Rape is an annual plant cultivated for its leaves and used as temporary pasture crop for livestock. Because of its deep taproot, it loosens soil and improves drainage, leaving the land friable and ready to grow a more useful crop. It helps to heal soils injured by overdoses of mineral fertilizer.

The succulent rape grows fast, producing best under cool, moist conditions. It also resists rather severe frosts and is best seeded in the fall in the southern states and in the spring in the northern ones.

Do not grow rape near hedge or field mustard since both will inhibit its growth.

Rice, Wild *(Zizania aquatica)*

This aquatic grass is not really rice at all, nor is it related to rice. It grows from four to eight feet tall in the shallow lakes of Minnesota, Wisconsin, and central Canada. There it has traditionally been harvested by Indians, who bend the heads of the plant over the edge of boats or canoes, beating the grains loose with two sticks.

Wild rice may be cultivated, growing best in quiet, pure water from one to six feet deep, along the margins of streams, ponds, and lakes or the floodplains of rivers with rich mud bottoms. It likes a slow current and will not grow in stagnant lakes or pools. A fairly shallow farm pond fed by streams can provide a good supply of this vitamin B–rich delicacy.

Do not try to plant the product you find in the grocery store, for only unhulled seed will sprout. Rice for planting must be sacked and kept wet. The seed may be planted by scattering over the surface of the water at the rate of a bushel per acre. The good seed will sink rapidly. If your area is small, use a large handful to a six-by-six-foot space. The best planting time is just before ice forms in late fall.

Rye *(Secale cereale)*

Rye is an excellent crop to choke out chickweed and other low-growing weeds that survive the winter. Planted twice in succession it even will choke out quack grass. A cover crop following sod will reduce black spot on strawberries and pink root on onions.

Rye will be benefited by cornflowers in the ratio of 100 to 1. A few pansies in the field will aid it, and the wild pansy (viola) will germinate almost 100 percent if grown nearby. Rye has an inhibiting effect on field poppy, retarding both the germination of the seed and its growth.

Rye flour sprinkled over cabbage plants while they are wet with morning dew will dehydrate cabbageworms and moths. Refined diatomaceous earth is useful as an insecticide for stored rye, but it is not injurious to warm-blooded animals.

Sorghum *(Andropogon sorghum; Sorghum vulgare* or *Holcus sorghum)*
Several insect-resistant strains of sorghum have been developed: 'Atlas' is resistant to the chinch bug, while 'Milo' is susceptible; 'Sudan' is resistant to the corn leaf aphid, while 'White Martin' is susceptible.

The sweet sorghums or sorgos are grown especially for the production of sorghum syrup, which is made by pressing the juice out of the stems. For the gardener who would like to be self-sufficient, here is a source of sweetening for his other foods. To get the maximum amount of sugar in the juice, sorghum should be seeded on soils that are not too fertile. Large vigorous stalks usually are lower in sugar than those grown more slowly and not over a half-inch in diameter.

Root exudates of sorghum apparently are poisonous to sesame and wheat. Stored sorghum grain can be kept free of insects by refined diatomaceous earth used as a desiccant dust.

Sudan grass (Sorghum vulgare sudanese) is a tall annual sorghum whose thin stalks grow quickly and may reach a height of 10 feet. It serves as excellent summer pasturage and grows well with soybeans if sufficient moisture is present.

Johnson grass (S. halepense), a perennial sorghum, grows as a weed in the southern United States. It resembles Sudan grass but spreads by creeping rootstocks in gardens or on land needed for cotton or other row crops to become a pest, but it makes excellent hay for cattle feed.

Soya Bean — Soybean *(Glycine max* and *G. soya)*

Soya beans, native to China, are so rich in protein they have been called the "meat without a bone." They are perhaps the world's oldest food crop, and they have meant meat, milk, cheese, bread, and oil to the Asiatic peoples for centuries. Like all legumes, they loosen and enrich poor soil and are an excellent crop to grow preceding others that need nitrogen. They grow faster and thicker than weeds and will choke them out.

Soya bean

Soybeans planted near corn protect it against chinch bugs and Japanese beetles. They grow well with black-eyed peas and will choke out weeds because they grow so rapidly.

Sugar Beet *(Beta vulgaris)*

Grain can be partially replaced as stock feed by sugar beets, which are liked by all animals and are good for increasing the milk flow of cows.

Cheat grass is often a despised weed but has the ability to quickly form a ground cover over denuded soil, preventing erosion. At the same time it replaces plants that are host to beet leafhopper, making it of considerable importance to sugar beet growers.

Timothy *(Phleum pratense)*

Timothy, a valuable, cool-season grass perennial, sometimes called herd's grass and by the English cat's-tail, has slender stems bearing round spikes of tiny, tightly packed flowers. Farmers in both Canada and the United States often sow timothy in rotation with oats and other grains. It does not last long when cattle or other animals graze on it continually, and is not considered a satisfactory pasture grass unless mixed with hardier types.

Timothy and other small grains are benefited by planting them with legumes such as alfalfa and sweet clover as a protection against white grubs.

Triticale *(Triticale)*

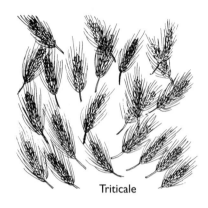

Triticale

The International Wheat and Maize Center of Mexico produced a new grain, triticale, by crossing wheat and rye, gaining the high yield of wheat and the disease- and drought-resistance of rye. This was accomplished by the tedious process of cross-fertilization among different species. By nurturing the resulting embryo and chemically causing its chromosomes to duplicate themselves, the scientists succeeded in producing fertile plants bearing the characteristics of both parents.

The name triticale (pronounced *trit-i-kay-lee*) derives from the scientific names for wheat and rye, *triticum* and *secale*. The cross has a higher protein content and protein efficiency ratio than either wheat or corn — comparable to soy concentrate — and it is also higher than wheat in lysine and methionine, two of the life-sustaining amino acids.

A delicious bread made from triticale is now obtainable in many grocery stores throughout the Southwest. The flour's baking qualities are better than rye's.

Triticale has shown the ability to produce two or three times as much per acre as either wheat or rye and can be grown anywhere in the world where wheat is found. The grain is being improved constantly as new strains are developed at various experiment stations throughout the country.

Vetch *(Vicia)*

Vetch, a relatively slow-growing perennial, is a good companion for oats and rye. Plant fast-growing rye or oats as a "nurse crop" to provide shade and check competitive growth. However, if this is done, the vetch should be planted more thinly than ordinarily or the annual nurse crop may be choked out by the sturdy perennial. Fall-planted vetch is one of our most valuable green manure crops. Being a legume, it enriches the soil with both nitrogen and humus.

Wheat *(Triticum vulgare)*

There are two stories about the origin of wheat, both extremely interesting. The first is that bread wheat appeared around 8000 B.C. when wild wheat by accidental cross-pollination apparently formed a hybrid with a type of "goat grass," resulting in much plumper grains. This new plant, called emmer, again crossed with goat grass, forming an even more luxuriant hybrid. Because the husk of this grain was so tight that the whole grain would not scatter to the wind as other grass seeds do, the continued existence of "wheat" was dependent upon man, and thus bread wheat came into being.

The Theosophists, however, believe that mankind at a certain stage in his development was assisted by some high initiates coming from the planet Venus. They believe that these advanced beings not only gave moral and social guidance to man but also brought with them wheat grains to supply a better cereal, bees to produce honey and fertilize flowers, and ants. Rye, they think, was produced by man in imitation of wheat by selective breeding. Oats and barley are thought to be hybrids brought about by crossing with earthly grasses.

In some regions, poppies spring up and become a weed in wheat fields. They should not be allowed to spread, for they check the wheat's growth. On the other hand, camomile is beneficial when permitted to grow with wheat in a very small ratio (1 to 100), while in larger amounts it is harmful. Wheat will be increased by the presence of corn.

The growth of wheat is adversely affected by cherry, dogwood, pine, and tulip, as well as proximity to the roots of sorghum. Canada thistle and field bindweed are harmful to both wheat and flax.

I have grown a good stand of winter wheat by sowing it in the fall on my Bermuda grass lawn. In our mild climate it grows intermittently all winter, heading about the last of June. After it is harvested, the Bermuda grass takes over again and you would never know the wheat had been there. I don't know whether this would work with other lawn grasses.

If you do make a sowing of winter wheat, avoid the Hessian fly by planting it late, timed according to when this fly appears in your area.

First Steps for Home Fruit Growing

For the gardener on a small lot, the site of the home orchard may be limited by necessity, the placement of trees being to a large extent dependent upon the overall landscape design. The homesteader, who has several acres, has at least a modest choice.

Since fruiting plants are more permanent than vegetables, their placement in the landscape design becomes most important. And often their usefulness may be doubled by considering also their ornamental and shade values.

Apples, plums, peaches, and pears are such beautiful flowering trees that they may be used for the same design scheme as crab apples, dogwoods, and redbuds. Pecans and walnuts (as well as apples and pears) make fine shade trees, too.

In areas where they grow well, blueberries will fit in nicely with other flowering shrubs such as forsythias, hydrangeas, and spiraeas. A trellis or arbor becomes both useful and beautiful if bunch grapes or muscadines are planted to grow on it. Unsightly fences may be covered or a patio comfortably shaded if a few grape plants are placed thereon.

Pollination, as applied to fruit and nut trees, vines, and bramble fruits, really is a matter of "companion planting," yet we seldom hear it called this.

Fruit and nut trees almost always do better if at least two of each kind are planted. For some varieties the need is imperative — they will bear scarcely at all without pollination help.

Few home gardens can accommodate more than two or three different kinds of fruit. To grow them successfully it is very important to consider varieties known to be self-fertile (also called self-fruitful), or known to be good pollinators for the other types you wish to grow. If your homesite is not large enough for many trees, check around the neighborhood and list the fruit and nut trees you find there. Some of them may be good pollinators for trees you would like to plant.

In this limited space I cannot possibly list every variety of each fruit that will ensure pollination, but there are a few general rules to follow for good results, and I have tried to include them in the chapters that follow. But remember that pollination, important as it is, is only one factor in success.

While I won't go into the details of cultural practices here, it should be said that trees in a healthy growing condition will naturally derive more benefit from correct companion plantings. Healthy trees produce more pollen. And this applies to all trees, whether standard or dwarf types.

Getting Started

If you have room to set aside a definite orchard area, the first year you should do subsoiling, plowing, disking, and grading well in advance of planting. If possible, choose a gently sloping site with good air and good soil drainage. There is nothing a tree dislikes more than hardpan and wet feet.

Soil that absorbs water readily is the best, and you can test this by digging a 10-inch-deep hole and filling it with water. If the hole drains completely within about eight hours, drainage may be considered satisfactory. However, if the water remains much longer, drainage is poor. To prevent root rot, work crushed rock, gravel, or peat moss into the soil. Mixing compost with the soil will help in more ways than one.

Grow a nourishing cover crop such as rye, vetch, or soya beans, and disk this in after well-rotted manure or compost has been spread. Allow time for its decomposition, for the trees do not like raw manure or organic matter around their roots. In a natural forest setting, raw organic matter remains on top and only decomposed humus touches the roots.

For shrubs or bramble fruits, the materials should be worked into the soil at least one foot deeper than planting depth. For trees, mix the additions to the soil about two or three feet deeper than the intended planting hole.

The actual planting of the trees comes after the soil has settled. Planting trees in early spring is the generally accepted practice, but in the South or Southwest it is often possible to plant with good results in fall or early winter.

Shortly before planting, fill the hole with water and allow it to drain completely. This will prevent the surrounding soil from absorbing most of the water applied to the freshly planted shrub or tree.

Maintaining a layer of mulch around new plantings helps their growth, since it preserves moisture and in time becomes compost, providing plant nutrients.

Culture

Dr. Ehrenfried E. Pfeiffer, author of *The Biodynamic Treatment of Fruit Trees, Berries and Shrubs,* believed that a mixed culture in the orchard as well as in the garden helped to keep down insect pests. He advocated growing nasturtiums between fruit trees as a means of transmitting a "flavor" to the tree that made it disagreeable to insects. He considered it particularly effective when the flowers were grown under apple trees to repel woolly aphids. A washing down of the trees with nasturtium juice was recommended, if planting them was not possible.

Dr. Pfeiffer also suggested for orchard use stinging nettle, chives, garlic (against borers), tansy, horseradish, and southernwood. Permanent covers considered beneficial are clovers, alfalfa, and pasture grasses. Temporary crops to turn under for green manure are such biennial clovers as mammoth clover, red clover, and incarnate clover. He believed buckwheat useful on a light, sandy soil.

Though a mixture of red clover and mustards is considered ideal, Dr. Pfeiffer cautioned that mustard, while it sweetens the soil, can become a rapidly spreading weed and for this reason should not be allowed to go to seed. Alfalfa hay, particularly if shredded or chopped, was thought to have special benefit as a mulch.

Dr. Pfeiffer also recommended a paste for all fruit trees consisting of equal parts of cow manure, diatomaceous earth, and clay, to which horsetail tea is added. This mixture is applied with a whitewash brush or with spraying equipment in the larger orchard.

A number of excellent preparations for fruit trees are obtainable from the Bio-Dynamic Farming and Gardening Association (see Sources).

More Hints for Fruit Growers

Here are some other helpful suggestions concerning fruiting plants:

- **Marigolds** planted near apple trees or between rows of nursery stock will benefit the trees used in grafting and budding.
- **Wild mustard** is beneficial to grapevines and fruit trees, but cut it before seeding.
- **Dandelions** in the area of fruits and flowers will stimulate them to ripen quickly.
- **Chives** improve the health of apple trees and will prevent apple scab. Use chive tea as a spray against apple scab and for powdery and downy mildew on gooseberries.
- **Pollination** is accomplished mainly by bees and other insects, so no sprays of any kind should be used at blossoming time.

- **Ripening apples** give off small amounts of ethylene gas, which sometimes limits the height of nearby plants but causes their flowers or fruit to mature earlier than normal.
- **Oats** may have an inhibitory effect on the growth of young apricot trees.
- If you must replace a **young fruit tree** on the same spot where an old one has been removed, choose a different variety.
- **Garlic juice** or the powdered extract contains a powerful anti-bacterial agent effective against diseases that damage stone fruits.
- Do not place **apples** near carrots in a root cellar, as they may cause the carrots to take on a bitter flavor. If apples and potatoes are stored near each other, both will develop an "off" flavor.
- **Nut trees** usually take a little longer to bear than fruit trees. While you are waiting for them to grow, interplant with peanuts (legumes). They will improve the soil and give you a crop as well.
- **Nut trees** are good to plant in pastures and near stables or manure and compost piles, to repel flies on cattle.

The Fungus Connection

One gardener reported that her unthrifty young peach trees apparently were assisted by moldy oats from the cleanings of the oat bin when one bushel was applied to each tree. After several weeks all her slow-growing trees were putting out new, healthy leaves.

A possible reason for the good growth of the peach trees is in the mold, rather than the oats, for almost all trees have a symbiotic relationship with some fungi (including molds). The fungi grow around the plant roots and furnish vitamins and other natural compounds necessary for a fast-growing and healthy tree.

This brings us back to the soil again. Because of this relationship, it's a good idea to have some of the original soil packed around the roots when transplanting a shrub or tree. Quite likely there will be fungi in the soil beneficial to the plant.

You may even do this: If you have a tree that isn't doing well after being set the first time, take some soil from another tree of the same variety that *is* growing well and dig it in around your problem tree. There's a good chance that your tree will perk up and grow.

This will work well not only with trees but also with other ornamentals and even with houseplants. If possible, investigate the original, invigorating habitat of such plants, remove some of the soil, and see if nature doesn't have a cure for the ailing plant far better than any commercial fertilizer you could buy.

Small Fruits

Blackberries (*Rubus* spp.)
Some self-unfruitful varieties of blackberries require cross-pollination. Others, even though self-fruitful, may benefit from the pollen-distributing visits of insects.

The flowers of blackberries are very attractive to their primary pollinators, honeybees. If a variety of blackberry is known to require cross-pollination, ensure a sufficient supply of pollinators in large acreages by placing colonies of bees in or near the field.

Do not grow blackberries near raspberries. Plant them in moderately acid soil, 5 to 5.7 pH.

Mulberries, chokecherries, and elderberries may be used to attract birds away from valued blackberry crops. Blackberries themselves are strong vital plants that help in preparing the soil to support the growth of trees.

Blueberries (*Vaccinium* spp.)
Have at least two different varieties — any two — in a blueberry planting.

Blueberries like very acid (4 to 5 pH) and open, porous soils, such as a mixture of sand and peat with loam. The water table should be 14 to 30 inches below the surface.

Boysenberry (*Rubus ursinis* 'Boysen')
Boysenberries are sometimes called trailing or semi-trailing blackberries.

Grapes (*Vitis* spp.)

Bunch grapes such as 'Concord', 'Fredonia', and 'Niagara' are self-fertile, and one vine will give an abundance of grapes even if planted alone. Grapes like a moderately acid soil of 5 to 5.7 pH. Perhaps more than any other fruiting plant, they need good air circulation to prevent fungus disease such as mildew. This is particularly important in moist, humid climates.

Grapes

Grapes in their natural environment swing high in the trees, doing especially well if the tree happens to be an elm or a mulberry. Such grapes are seldom troubled by either brown rot or mildew. Since growing grapes in trees is impractical for most, the best solution is perhaps a terraced hillside unsuitable for other crops.

Try planting hyssop with your grapes for an increased yield, or use legumes as an intercrop. Cypress spurge is unfriendly, so do not let it grow nearby. To discourage the rose chafer, keep grass out of the vineyard, since its larvae feed on grass roots.

(See also *Muscadine* below.)

Muscadine

As natives of the southeastern United States, muscadines do well under the high temperature and humidity found in this area, but they also are resistant to drought conditions and disease. Under favorable conditions they will live many years, but are not hardy in the northern United States. Some varieties are self-pollinating, while others require a pollenizer.

Raspberries (*Rubus* spp.)

Raspberries, which like a near-neutral soil (6.5 to 7 pH), are self-fertile.

Because of virus disease, black and purple raspberries should be planted no closer than 600 feet from red varieties. Do not grow raspberries and blackberries near each other, either. Do not plant any raspberries near potatoes, since they make the potatoes more susceptible to blight.

Strawberry *(Fragaria x ananassa)*
Almost all strawberries now sold, both June-bearing and everbearing, are self-fruitful. The "best" varieties vary from one area to another.

A cover crop of rye following sod will reduce the incidence of black rot on strawberries. They do well in combination with bush beans and spinach.

Strawberries will benefit if a few plants of borage, also a good attractant for honeybees, are grown near the bed. Lettuce is good used as a border. Pyrethrum, planted alongside, serves well as a pest preventative. A spruce hedge also is protective. White hellebore will control sawfly, and marigolds are useful, too, if you suspect the presence of nematodes.

Pine needles alone or mixed with straw make a fine mulch, said to make the berries taste more like the wild variety. Spruce needles also may be used as a mulch, but my personal preference is chopped alfalfa hay.

In some areas, growers plant strawberries as an intercrop in peach, apple, fig, orange, or other tree-fruit orchards. When the orchard is first planted, strawberries may be set out and grown for several years before the trees need all the ground. The strawberries furnish some income from the land, or at least pay the expense of caring for the orchard. The intensive cultivation given strawberries is especially good for young orchards. Also, because strawberries do not bear well unless moisture conditions are good, they will prove a good indicator of the orchard conditions.

Tree Fruits

Apples *(Malus* spp.)
Only a few apples will bear well if grown alone, producing a good crop from self-pollination. Most should not be planted alone or be depended upon for pollination in a combination; they are either low or lacking in viable pollen. Suppliers of fruit trees have

information available on which combinations work best, and you should be sure you understand the needs of any tree you plan to buy.

If you have room only for one tree, there is still a way that you can have your favorite apple and pollinate it too. Graft a branch of a good pollinator somewhere on the host tree and this will serve your purpose. Apples like a near-neutral soil with a pH of 6.5 to 7.

Apricots (*Prunus* spp.)

All apricots are self-fertile, but they will benefit from cross-pollination to bear more heavily.

Cherries (*Prunus* spp.)

All sour pie cherries are self-fruitful and have no pollination problems. A single tree may be planted and expected to produce well from its own pollen.

Sweet cherries all are self-unfruitful and will require another variety nearby to enable them to set fruit. To further complicate things, there are even instances of pollen incompatibility among this group. A good nursery will give you information on pollination needs of the trees you are interested in.

Wheat is suppressed by the roots of cherry trees, and potatoes grown in the vicinity are less resistant to blight.

Citrus (*Citrus* spp.)

Lime, lemon, orange, and grapefruit trees grow better in the area of guava, live oak, or rubber trees, which apparently exert a protective influence.

Crab Apples (*Malus* spp.)

Crab apple trees are often planted simply for their beauty. But they are self-fertile, and a good variety such as 'Dolgo' will provide both beauty and fruit.

Fig (*Ficus carica*)

Many people consider figs a tropical fruit, but there are varieties that will do well elsewhere. The fruit of the fig tree is peculiar in

Fig

that the flowers form inside the fruit's skin. Pokeweed grows well as a fig's companion.

Most figs offered by general nurseries are self-fertile, but some varieties will not mature their fruits unless the tiny female flowers are fertilized by pollen from a special kind of fig tree called a caprifig. Other varieties bear larger fruit if they are subjected to this process, which is known as caprification. The pollen is transferred by a tiny wasp that spends part of its life in the fruits of the caprifig. In regions where Smyrna and other figs requiring caprification are grown, caprifigs are planted also.

Mulberries (*Morus* spp.)

Mulberry trees have rather insipid-tasting fruits but can be very useful to lure birds away from cherries and berry plants. The birds seem actually to prefer mulberries.

The Russian mulberry (*Morus alba* 'Tatarica'), a rapid-growing tree, bears an abundant crop resembling blackberries, which may be made up into pies and jams.

Nectarine *(Prunus persica var. nucipersica)*

Nectarines are self-fruitful. They also will pollinate peaches, and peaches nearby will help the nectarine to set a larger crop.

Peach *(Prunus persica)*

Most peaches are self-fruitful, but a few require a pollinator (which can be any other variety of peach). Peaches like a near-neutral soil with a pH from 6.5 to 7.

Never plant a young peach tree where an old one has been removed — plant a different fruit tree.

If peach leaf curl appears and only a few leaves are affected, pull them off by hand. Feeding the tree with well-rotted manure or compost high in nitrogen will help the tree back to health. Garlic planted close to the trunk will protect against borers.

Pears (*Pyrus* spp.)

Almost all pears require other varieties nearby for a good fruit set, the exceptions under most conditions being 'Duchess' and 'Kieffer', which are self-fruitful.

'Bartlett' and 'Seckel' are not compatible, and 'Kieffer' is not always a good pollinator for 'Bartlett'.

If you live in an area where fire blight prevails, it will pay you to plant resistant varieties.

Some orchardists believe that pears are suppressed by the root excretions of grass, but a successful pear grower in California, believing the opposite, lets a variety of grasses and weeds grow in his orchard.

This same grower sprays against codling moth and leaf roller, using ryania because it is specific, killing only chewing insects. As a fertilizer he uses chicken manure to provide nitrogen, plus other animal manures, cottonseed meal, compost, and dried blood.

Persimmons (*Diospyros* spp.)

There are two species of importance. The first, American persimmon *(Diospyros virginiana)*, is native to a large part of the United States, and the second, the Oriental or Japanese persimmon *(Diospyros kaki)*, is a native of China and Korea. American and Japanese trees are not interfruitful. Persimmons come in dozens of cultivated varieties, which are considered superior to the wild type.

Persimmon

The common persimmon is a small, low-growing tree perfectly adapted for the homeowner with limited space, since it ordinarily attains a height no greater than 40 or 50 feet. The inconspicuous, greenish yellow, urn-shaped male and female flowers are borne on separate trees.

A number of excellent grafted persimmon varieties are offered by the Louis Gerardi Nursery. (See Sources.)

Plums (*Prunus* spp.)

Almost all plums require pollination, though there are a few that will fruit alone. Plums like a moderately acid soil of 5 to 5.7 pH.

Quince *(Cydonia oblonga)*

Quince trees are self-fruitful.

Nuts

Almond *(Prunus dulcis)*

The almond is not a true nut but belongs to the Rose family. All varieties produce better if pollen from another tree is available. Peaches and almonds, being of the same family, will pollinate each other.

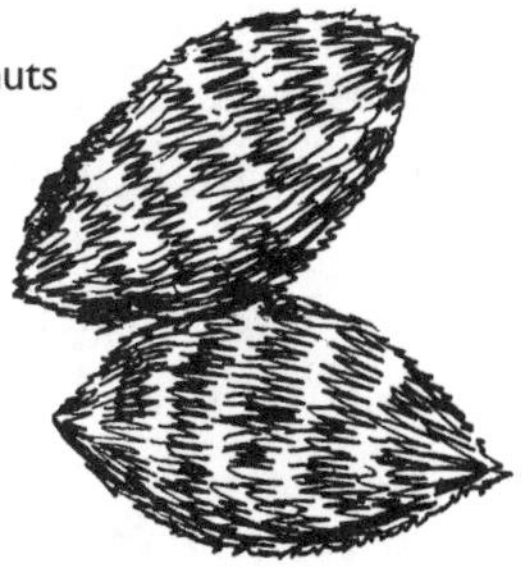

Butternuts

Butternut *(Juglans cinerea)*

Butternut has an inhibitory effect on plants within its immediate vicinity, but to a lesser degree than the black walnut. (See *Walnut* entries.)

Cashew *(Anacardium occidentale)*

This native of Brazil has become naturalized in many tropical countries and will grow on sandy soils in Florida. Cross-pollination is not necessary.

Chestnut, American *(Castanea dentata)*

The chestnut blight has just about wiped out the native American species. However, much work has been done to develop disease-resistant varieties, and a revival of this tree is in progress.

Chestnut, Chinese *(Castanea mollissima)*
Plant two or more varieties for cross-pollination.

Filberts and Hazels *(Corylus* spp.)
In ancient times many believed that a forked hazel twig had super-
natural powers. Such twigs are mentioned in the Bible, while the
Romans also describe the magical
quality of the branches and told  Hazelnuts
of hazel divining rods being
used to find water and pre-
cious minerals underground.
Hazels furnish valuable
cover and food for wildlife.
Homeowners also plant
them as ornamentals or to shelter other plants. In some forests
hazels form such dense thickets that tree seedlings cannot grow
and heavy machinery is needed to uproot them so more valuable
timber can be planted.
Hazel trees and bushes are beneficial in pastures and elsewhere
against flies. Cows like to nibble on the leaves, which increase the
butterfat in their milk, while the tannic acid also acts as a cleansing
agent for their digestive systems.
It is recommended that two varieties be planted for cross-
pollination and better crops.

Hickories *(Carya* spp.)
The hickories, like the walnuts, have male and female flowers growing separately on the same shoot of the current season's growth.
Many varieties appear to be self-unfruitful, so it is good practice to
plant several varieties together to ensure cross-pollination.

Pecan *(Carya illinoinensis)*
These trees in all their varieties give no evidence of cross-
incompatibility, and all will bear larger crops if two or more
varieties are planted together.

Pecan trees like plenty of nitrogen. In the orchard, plant a winter and spring cover crop such as clover, which harbors nitrogen-fixing bacteria. For a lawn specimen, let a dense mat of grass grow near the trunk to conserve soil moisture and prevent sunscald of the roots. It is good to mulch with grass clippings, too.

Pecans

The casebearer and hickory shuck-worm, the most serious pecan pests, are best foiled by releasing trichogramma wasps in the orchard. Do not store pecan meats near onions or oranges.

Walnut, Black *(Juglans nigra)*

Grafted varieties of these self-fruitful trees usually produce each year, while wild trees generally produce well only in alternate years, some only every third year.

Black walnut trees are known to produce a substance called juglone, which is washed from the leaves to the soil, inhibiting the growth of many plants within the area where the trees grow. Cultivated plants not compatible with black walnuts are apples, alfalfa, potatoes, tomatoes, blackberries, azaleas, rhododendrons, and heathers. The butternut also seems to have this quality, but plants near it are less severely affected. (See also *Sycamore* in the Trees and Shrubs chapter.)

Toxicity is contained in the roots of black walnuts as well as in the leaves, and because of this many plants will not grow near the tree. But not all are discouraged. Right at the drip line of a black walnut I have a bed of rainbow-colored iris, interplanted with daylilies, grape

Walnuts

hyacinths, and daffodils, none of which appear to be in the least affected.

Drawbacks aside, the black walnut is prized for its valuable wood and delicious nuts. In addition, the tree's leaves scattered around the house or put in the dog kennel will repel fleas.

A Russian remedy to prevent sunburn is to rub freshly ground walnut leaves on the skin. The dark juice of walnut hulls applied to ringworm is said to heal the scalp. (See also *Walnuts, English*, below.)

Walnut, English *(Juglans regia)*

Unless you live in a favorable climate, you will probably be more successful with a tree of the Carpathian type, which will do well farther north.

Walnuts are monoecious — that is, the male and female blossoms are separate on the same tree. They are self-fertile but produce better in plantings of several nearby.

English walnuts do not have the level of detrimental leaf and root excretions found in black walnuts, but their shade makes it difficult to grow some plants nearby. Many of the fruit mints, such as apple, orange, pineapple, and spearmint, will do well, however, as will angelica, sweet anise, and other herbs that like filtered sunlight.

Ornamental Trees and Shrubs

Alder *(Alnus tenufolia)*

Closely related to the hornbeams and birches is this small, water-loving tree that grows very rapidly and serves definite, special uses. The genus *Alnus* includes 20 species, nine of which grow in North America and six of which reach the height of trees. Alders may be planted in hedges along the borders of streams where their closely interlacing roots hold the banks from crumbling and keep the current clear in midstream. Like willows, alders are of assistance in draining wet soils.

In America the black alder *(Ilex verticillata)* is often found in horticultural varieties. The daintiest are the cut-leaved forms, of which *imperialis,* with leaves fingered like a white oak, is a good example. The root nodules add nitrogen to the soil, the black alder being the only nonleguminous plant that is able to perform this function. (See *Legumes* in the Soil Improvement chapter.)

Azalea *(Rhododendron)*

Azaleas, holly, pieris, and rhododendrons are good companions for a landscape planting because all like humusy, acid soil. Do not plant azaleas or rhododendrons near black walnut trees. The substance called juglone washed from the leaves of black walnuts is detrimental to them.

Beech *(Fagus)*

Beech trees and ferns often grow together, and scilla bulbs do well under the trees. Beech trees in their infancy do well under the shade of other trees, so each fruiting tree is the mother of many young ones.

Birch *(Betula)*

It is believed that birch roots excrete substances that encourage fermentation and make the trees useful to plant around manure and compost piles. Dr. Ehrenfried Pfeiffer, one of the early advocates of the biodynamic method of farming and gardening, observed that composts fermented in the vicinity of the gray birch derived benefit from it and suffered no losses of nutrients even if the roots actually penetrated the heap. It is considered best, though, to maintain a distance of at least six feet from the tree when building a compost pile.

Conifers

Turpentine substances washing from the leaves of conifers such as pine trees will inhibit the fermentation process of compost piles. Interplanting onions with conifers will help prevent damage by squirrels, which eat the buds of Scotch, white, and red pines. Winter-hardy Egyptian onions are the best kind.

Pine needles make an attractive mulch and will increase the stem strength, flavor, and productiveness of strawberries. In general, conifers have an adverse

Squirrel damage in pines and other trees can be limited by planting onions nearby.

effect on the growth of wheat, since rain washing over them picks up substances that inhibit the germination of seeds.

Elderberry *(Sambucus nigra* and *Sambucus canadensis)*
Elderberries, having a liking for moist soil, are helpful near compost yards that are difficult to drain, and will also assist in the fermentation of the compost. Elderberries are noted for their ability to produce very fine humus soil about their roots.

Elm *(Ulmus)*
Grapevines that climb trees, swinging high in the air, are greatly benefited by good air circulation and sunlight. It is the sunlight on their leaves rather than on the grapes that causes them to ripen to perfection. Elm trees are particularly beneficial as supports for grapevines.

The slippery elm *(U. fulva)* is also known as the red elm because its wood is red and the moose elm because moose are fond of browsing its young shoots. When the bark is stripped from this valuable tree, it is possible to scrape from its inner surface the thick, fragrant, mucilaginous cambium — a delectable substance that allays both hunger and thirst. The inner bark, dried, ground, and mixed with milk, is a valuable food for invalids. Fevers and acute inflammatory disorders have been treated with the bark, and poultices of the bark also relieve throat and chest ailments.

Hedges
Hedges used as windbreaks are of particular value in dry, windy areas. Blueberries make a delightful hedge where they can be grown. Rosa rugosa makes an almost impenetrable hedge and also affords a harvest of vitamin-rich rose hips. 'Cardinal' autumn olive *(Elaeagnus umbellata* 'Cardinal') and dwarf burning bush *(Euonymus alatus compactus)* are beloved by birds, as is red-leaf barberry *(Berberis thunbergii atropurpurea)*. For brilliant color there are 'Golden Prince' euonymus *(Euonymus fortunei)* and 'Goldflame' spiraea *(Spiraea bumalda)*.

Locust (*Robinia* spp.)

Sweet pea–type blossoms on a tree, or pods like the pea's swinging from the twigs, mean that it's a member of the pod-bearing Leguminosae family, to which both herbaceous and woody plants belong.

The black locusts *(R. pseudacacia)* have nectar-laden, white flowers of "butterfly form," which honeybees (leading a host of other insects) swarm about as long as a flower remains to offer its sweet nectar. Cross-fertilization is the advantage the tree gains from all it gives.

Locust, good to plant as a border, has leaves, roots, and bark that are poisonous if eaten, but the pods of honey locust *(Gleditsia triacanthos)* contain a sweetish pulp used as cattle feed and occasionally eaten by small boys, who brave the tree's thorns to get them.

Being a leguminous tree, the black locust is a good companion to lima beans.
There are toxins dangerous to humans in the leaves, bark, and roots, however.

Maple *(Acer)*

The single genus *Acer* includes from 60 to 70 species widely distributed over North America. *Acer saccharum,* the sugar maple, is the best known and economically the most important for both its beautiful wood and its sap, which yields maple syrup. The black maple *(A. nigrum)* is the sugar maple of South Dakota and Iowa. Red maple *(A. rubrum),* perhaps the most beautiful of all, is a swamp lover but will thrive on hillsides if the soil is moist. It is widely planted in parks and along streets.

Maples have shallow, spreading root systems and it is difficult to get other plants to grow near them. They may also excrete substances that inhibit the growth of some plants, particularly wheat. Maple leaves laid in layers between apples, carrots, potatoes, and other root vegetables have a preservative effect.

Mulberry *(Morus alba, M. rubra, M. nigra)*

White mulberry is the chosen food of silkworms and no substitute has ever topped this tree's preeminence. The berries of the red mulberry *(M. rubra)* do not compare with the cultivated type, but are of value in poultry yards and hog pastures, where they are eagerly devoured. The black mulberry *(M. nigra),* believed a native of Persia, has large, dark red, juicy fruits but is hardy only in the southern and Pacific Coast states, where it is a desirable tree because it is so attractive to birds.

Mulberry trees are particularly good as a support for grapes. Tree-grown grapes are more difficult to pick than trellised grapes, but they will be relatively free of fungus diseases due to better circulation of air around them. Worms in horses may be repelled by mulberry leaves, and Russian mulberry is sometimes used as a trap crop to protect cherries and strawberries.

Nurse Trees

As abandoned fields again become covered with vegetation, the brushland is gradually reforested. The first trees are quick-growing, short-lived types that provide conditions suitable for the slower-growing, longer-lived trees. Looking at the forest floor, you will see very few pine seedlings. Other seedlings — young oaks, black cherries, and hickories — do better. Gradually the pines will die off and the young hardwoods grow up and take their place. Should a forest fire occur, the whole process will start over again.

Nitrogen-Fixing Trees

Pod-bearing (leguminous) trees have the power to take nitrogen out of the air and store it in their roots and stems. The decay of these parts restores to the soil the plant food that is most often lacking and most expensive to replace. These trees and shrubs include black locust *(Robinia pseudacacia);* bristly locust *(Robinia hispida),* sometimes called rose-acacia; clammy locust *(Tobinia viscosa);* Scotch broom *(Robinia scopariua);* honey locust *(Gleditsia triacanthos);* Kentucky coffee tree *(Gymnocladus dioicus);* redbud *(Cercis canadensis),* sometimes called Judas tree; yellowwood *(Cladrastis lutea);* woad waxes *(Genista tinctoria),* sometimes called dyer's greenweed; indigo bush *(Amorpha fruticosa),* sometimes called false indigo; mesquite *(Prosopis juliflora),* screwbean *(Prosopis pubescens),* a slender-trunked mesquite, sometimes called screwpod; Palo Verde acacia *(Cercidium torreyanum);* Jamaica dogwood *(Icthyomethia piscipula);* horse bean *(Parkinsonia aculeata);* Texas ebony *(Zigia flexicaulis);* and frijolito *(Sophora secundiflora).*

Black alder *(Ilex verticillata)* also adds nitrogen to the soil. It is the only known nonleguminous shrub with root nodules that can do this. (See *Alder* in this chapter.)

Oak *(Quercus)*

Oaks grown with American chestnuts seem to give them some resistance to chestnut blight. During their growth, oaks accumulate a large amount of calcium in their bark, yet amazingly the most calcium has been found in the ash of oak trees that grew in calcium-deficient soil.

A mulch of oak leaves serves to control radish and turnip maggots as well as repelling slugs, cutworms, and grubs of June bugs, but some gardeners believe the leaves have an inhibiting effect on certain vegetables. Therefore they should be fully composted before being spread on the garden.

In Germany it has long been a practice to control greenhouse pests such as ants, aphids, and small mites with the smoke from oak leaves. The smoke is not considered poisonous and will not kill bacteria in the soil, nor leave harmful residues.

Live oaks are believed to exert a protective influence on citrus trees.

The trichogramma wasp, whose larvae feed on moth eggs, helps keep oak trees green by controlling gypsy moths. *Bacillus thuringiensis* (see the Pest Control chapter) will also control and kill various caterpillars on the trees.

Osage Orange *(Maclura pomifera)*

This thorny tree is native from Arkansas to Texas and is hardy as far north as New England and central New York. It is valued for windbreaks or to grow in poor soils, and is an excellent hedge plant, being almost impenetrable when fully mature. It was widely planted by the pioneers as a living fence around their homes before barbed wire came into use. The name refers to the Osage Indians and to the yellow fruit, which looks like an orange but is inedible.

Pine *(Pinus)*

Pine boughs are good to lay over peonies in winter for protection. Remove them in the spring before growth starts. Pine needles make a good mulch for azaleas, rhododendrons, and other acid-loving plants and will increase vigor and flavor in strawberries.

Pine needles contain terpene, which, washed down by rain, has an inhibiting effect on seed germination. It is not good to place a compost heap near pine trees.

Poplar *(Populus)*

The quick-growing, short-lived poplar often fulfills the function of "nurse tree." When a fire sweeps through the forest, it is likely to be the first tree to grow again on the bare land. The poplar's abundant seed, much like willow's, is wind-sown far and wide. Lombardy poplars, which look like exclamation points, are often planted to shelter other plants from the wind.

In Canada, very good stock feed has been made by boiling poplar wood under pressure.

Rosa Rugosa *(Rosa)*

This "hippy" rose has become so famous that it deserves to be mentioned all by itself. Grown in a mass, it makes a charming windbreak as well as an almost impenetrable barrier for animals. It grows better with purslane, parsley, and mignonette around it; is protected from rose bugs by alliums or onions nearby. Keep boxwood away. It blooms prolifically and is an excellent source for berries (hips) rich in vitamin C, containing more than oranges. The hips are used for making teas, jams, soups, and other dishes.

Rosa rugosa

Rose *(Rosa)*

All the alliums — garlic, onions, chives, and shallots — are beneficial to roses, protecting them against black spot, mildew, and aphids. For a recipe to overcome black spot in roses, see *Tomatoes* in the Vegetables chapter.

Garlic and onions are particularly beneficial to roses. In Bulgaria, where attar of roses is produced for perfumes, it is a common practice to interplant them with roses since they cause the roses to produce a stronger perfume in larger quantities.

Roses also are aided by parsley against rose beetles, by onions to repel rose chafers, by mignonette as a ground cover, and by lupines to increase soil nitrogen and attract earthworms. Marigolds are helpful against nematodes, and geraniums or milky spore disease against Japanese beetle. (See *Milky Spore Disease* in the Pest Control chapter.)

A carpet of low-growing weeds from the Purslane family will improve the spongy soil around the roots of rosebushes. An infusion of elderberry leaves in lukewarm water sprinkled over roses is thought to control caterpillar damage and is also recommended for blight.

Do not plant roses with other plants that have woody, out-spreading roots that will compete with the roses for soil nutrients.

Sassafras *(Sassafras albidum)*

Sassafras is sometimes called the mitten tree from its peculiar leaves, which grow in three different shapes: the simple ovate leaf, a larger blade (oval in form but with one side extended and lobed to form a thumb), and third, a symmetrical three-lobed leaf, the pattern of a narrow mitten with a thumb on each side.

Sassafras

Sassafras will repel mosquitoes. The pungent oil has antiseptic properties, and the bark mixed with dried fruit wards off insects.

A tea made from the bark of young sassafras roots has been used for digestive disturbances. The dried leaves, called file, were formerly much used in the southern states as an ingredient in soups. However, sassafras is now regarded as unsafe for internal use.

Spruce *(Picea)*

Three species of woodpeckers were credited with controlling a serious infestation of spruce beetles in Colorado in 1947. Naturally occurring *Bacillus thuringiensis* (see the Pest Contol chapter) has been found to give good control of this beetle in some forests.

Sycamore *(Platanus occidentalis)*

Studies conducted by American and Iraqi scientists show that sycamores inhibit the growth of other herbaceous plant species, and the decaying leaves cause significant reduction in seed germination and seedling growth. Organic compounds leached from the leaves often are allelopathic to plants, and virtually no herbaceous plants will grow under the trees.

Sycamore bark has value, however. Boiled in water and made into a poultice, it is good to use for poison ivy.

Wild Cherry *(Prunus pensylvanica)*

The wild bird, pine, or red cherry grows from Newfoundland to Georgia and west to the Rocky Mountains in rocky woods, forming thickets that are valuable as nurse trees. Wild cherry often springs up in burned-over districts where its bird-sown pits take root, the young trees sheltering new pines and hardwoods. It provides berries for birds and nectar-laden flowers for bees, so it can scarcely be called worthless, even though it is a short-lived tree.

The wild black cherry *(P. serotina)* is sometimes called the rum cherry. A tonic is derived from its bark, roots, and fruit, and brandies and cordials are made from its heavy-clustered fruits, which hang until late summer, turning black and losing their astringency when fully ripe. The wild black cherry makes an attractive shade and park tree, too.

The wild black cherry and the chokecherry *(P. virginiana)* are both of value to attract birds. Unfortunately, the tent caterpillar favors them to lay its eggs, making the trees unpopular with farmers. The egg rings in the outer smaller branches are easily seen and removed.

Willow *(Salix)*

The tough and fibrous roots of willow are useful in binding the banks of streams that may erode. Nature seems to have designed them specifically for this purpose, for wherever a twig lies upon the ground, it will strike root at every joint if the soil is sufficiently moist. The wind often breaks off twigs and the water carries them downstream where they lodge on banks and sandbars, which soon become covered with billows of green.

For thousands of years the bark and leaves of the willow have yielded resins and juices that eased the aches and pains of rheumatism and neuralgia or alleviated the distress of fevers. In the 1820s, salicin, the active principle of willow bark, was isolated, and in 1897 a synthetic derivative gave the world aspirin.

Windbreaks

Before planting a windbreak, study your land carefully and plan to put it where it will do the most good. Consider prevailing wind directions and the location and relationship of your buildings to the area you want protected. Most often windbreaks are planted across the west and north sides of a property, but of course there are exceptions to this rule, depending on the configuration of the land and the winds.

Do not plant your screen too close to the garden, for if the windbreak is to consist of trees and shrubs, they will rob the soil of moisture and nutrients. If you have sufficient land, plant the windbreak at least 50 feet from field crops. Very possibly you do not have this much room, but be as generous as you can.

The protective factor of a windbreak is 20 times its height. Thus a 10-foot screen would give you protection up to 200 feet downwind from it. You will also receive protection for several feet in front of the tree belt because it causes the air to back up and act as an invisible wall before it hits the planting of trees. Not the least of its uses is to hold down soil against heavy winds and to keep snow from drifting over walks and driveways. It may even help you to reduce fuel bills.

In the prairie regions in particular, shelterbelt plantings have a marked influence on local climate, especially if they are placed at right angles to prevailing winds. A chain of such belts checks movement of the air, slowing down the wind velocity even before the windbreak is reached, and starts up a whole series of favorable climatic influences. These influences, such as a reduction of evaporation by increasing the humidity of the air, improve the yield of crops grown under their protection. (See *Hedges* in this chapter, and *Vertical Gardening* in Garden Techniques.)

Witch Hazel *(Hamamelis virginiana)*

The witch hazel is a stout, many-stemmed shrub or small tree, characteristically an undergrowth of larger trees. Native Americans were the first to use the bark of the witch hazel for curing inflammations. An infusion of the twigs and roots is made by boiling them for 24 hours in water to which alcohol then is added. The extract distilled from this mixture is used for bruises and sprains and to allay the pain of burns.

Perhaps the alcohol is the effective agent, for chemists have failed to discover any medicinal properties in either bark or leaf — yet who knows, they may still find it.

The tree has the peculiar property of throwing its seeds, particularly in dry, frosty weather. This does for the parent tree what the winged seeds of other, taller trees accomplish.

Witch hazel gets its name from the fact that superstitious English miners once used the forked twigs as divining rods.

Garden Techniques

Border Plants

Castor beans planted around the perimeter of the garden will repel moles, while borders of daffodil, narcissus, scilla, and grape hyacinth around flower beds will discourage mice. If used in small amounts, dead nettle (henbit), sainfoin, esparsette, hyssop, lemon balm, and valerian are helpful to all vegetables. Yarrow is a good plant in paths, as well as borders, as it will grow well even if walked upon. Planted as a border to the herb garden, it enhances the growth of essential oils in the herbs.

Catch Cropping

This simply means growing a quick-to-mature crop of some vegetable in ground you've reserved for a planting of a later or slower-growing crop such as tomatoes, or a member of the Cabbage family such as broccoli or cauliflower. While you are waiting, put in radishes, lettuce, or spinach as a catch crop.

Climate

Since climates vary greatly throughout the world, where you live should always be taken into account when you plan your garden.

Maximum summer and minimum winter temperature should be considered, as well as annual rainfall.

For best success, try plants recommended for your area, making these your garden basics. This determined, you can then have fun experimenting each year with a few borderline plants those that do best in either a warmer or colder climate. Often, by providing shelter or otherwise creating a "mini" climate you may grow these successfully. Winter protection will help in the North, shade or a windbreak in the South. Some natural feature of your land, such as a pond, may enable you to grow something that your neighbor a few miles away cannot. (See *Microclimate* in this chapter.)

Mulching to keep the ground cool may be helpful for certain plants. Improving soil with humus often makes it possible to grow vegetables or plants that formerly were unsuccessful.

Damping-Off

This is a disease caused by fungi, apparently present in the soil, that kills many young plants. It is characterized by collapse of the stems, or the seedlings falling over. It may occur before the seeds germinate or after the seedlings emerge. To avoid this, you can start seeds in a commercial soilless medium; but if you make your own potting soil in which seeds are to be planted, it should be treated to kill the fungi by steam-heating to 180°F for half an hour or more.

A simple method for the home gardener is dry-heating the soil in an oven. Place the soil 4 to 5 inches deep in a pan and bury a small potato about 1½ inches in diameter in it. Bake in 200°F oven until the potato is done and the soil is sterilized and ready to use.

French Intensive Gardening

This type of gardening, which stresses maximum use of the soil and first became popular in the 1800s, is largely accomplished by using raised beds. These may be any length but narrow enough to permit easy handling from either side. Raised beds have the advantage of improved drainage and better aeration. The soil does not become waterlogged in winter and as a result it warms up faster in spring and produces earlier crops.

Prepare the soil by loosening to a depth of 12 inches and removing all weeds. Add compost or well-decomposed manure as well as any other organic amendments (agricultural lime, gypsum, bonemeal, phosphate rock, etc.) that a soil test may indicate. Double digging is then done. This means that where the first spade-depth of soil is removed, a second spade-depth of soil is loosened before soil from the top layer is replaced.

If you are working with extremely poor soil, the bottom spade-depth may need to have additional incorporations of sand, compost, and loamy soil. All this sounds like a lot of work, and it is, but as the soil is improved each year, the work gets easier.

The benefit derived from this intensive gardening method is the increased number of plants that may be grown in a very small

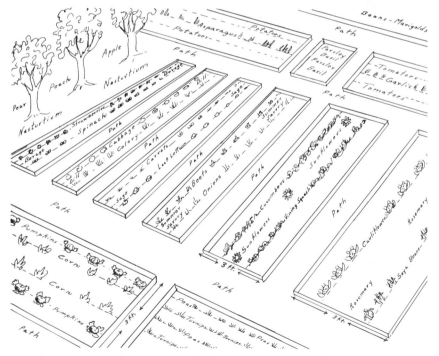

French intensive gardening is an ideal way to save space and to use companion planting effectively.

area. Perhaps in no other form of gardening is companion planting so important, since herbs and vegetables are so closely crowded together.

In general, the smaller vegetables and salad greens are best suited to this type of culture, but there is no law that says you can't grow corn and pumpkins and sunflowers and cucumbers this way if you want to!

Frost

Vegetables frequently are classified according to their ability to survive frosts. The U.S. Department of Agriculture defines the differences:

Hardy or cool-season crops will survive medium to heavy frosts. Seed from this group (peas, beets, kale, etc.) can be planted as soon as the soil can be prepared in the spring, or in midsummer for a late-fall crop.

Semi-hardy vegetables will survive a light frost. Seed will germinate at relatively low temperatures, and can be planted 2 to 3 weeks before the last frost date. This necessarily will vary in different sections of the country.

Tender or warm-season crops (tomatoes, eggplant, bell pepper, etc.) are injured or killed by frost, and their seeds seldom germinate in cold soil.

Honeybee *(Apis mellifera)*

Both in the garden and in the orchard, honeybees are an important agent of pollination. They are particularly attracted to the often inconspicuous flowers of herb plants.

A hive of bees is a good weather indicator, for if drones are forced out of the hive during fair weather, it is a sign that cold, wet weather is imminent.

When hiving a new swarm of bees, rub the hive's inside with lemon balm, which the bees like. A smoke from jimsonweed (datura) calms the bees when a hive is opened.

Intercropping

This is really the heart of companion planting, for the idea is to have two or more different vegetables growing on the same piece of ground, or in the same row, providing diversification. And this idea need not be confined to vegetables. Flowers and herbs can happily bump shoulders with each other. In fact, they *should.*

If your garden is small and you don't want to have empty spaces between your peas and bean rows, intercrop with broccoli, Brussels sprouts, cabbages, cauliflower, kale, or even radishes or carrots. After the early peas and beans are out, the slower-growing vegetables have all the space to themselves, and you have room to walk again. This may make things a bit cramped at times, but if you have little space and a short growing season, it's well worth trying. Of course, to be successful you must keep up the fertility of your soil.

I like to keep a sort of "floating crop game" going in my own garden, making small plantings of quick-growing vegetables that sprout readily from seed, such as lettuce, radish, spinach, celery, cabbage, kale, chard, collards, and other greens. Staggered plantings mean fresh supplies coming on all through the season.

Plants that will help each other are put together as often as possible, either in the same row (for instance, marigolds with bush beans) or in adjacent rows. Lettuce and onions do well together, so I pop in a lettuce plant each time I pull a green onion for the table. I plant onions close together and pull every other one, letting the remaining onions mature for dry onions. In my climate even eggplant and green peppers benefit from a bit of shade, so I plant these together in a row next to okra.

Many vine crops, such as squash, cucumbers, and pumpkins, grow well with corn and may even protect it from raccoons. The corn is helpful in protecting vine crops from wilt. Many early crops do well following spinach, which is rich in saponin. (See

Saponin in the Soil Improvement chapter.) Early spinach also may be intercropped with strawberries.

Many vegetables are pretty enough to put in the flower beds. Parsley between bulbs provides an attractive background in the spring. Tomatoes can grow with roses and at the same time protect them against black spot.

Chive clumps are another attractive planting for the rose garden (see *Chive* in the Herbs chapter for benefits). They grow larger each year, late spring bringing a pincushion of lavender blossoms that last for many days.

Hardy amaryllis, a member of the Lily family, sends out long strap leaves in early spring. After the leaves ripen and die, the ground is bare until August, when a sturdy stem emerges to grow quickly and bear fragrant pink lilies. A lettuce planting between the bulbs contrasts with the flower, making it far more beautiful.

Some vegetables have been especially hybridized for oramentation in a flower planting. Flowering cabbage and kale come in colorful shades of red, white, and green, yet have excellent flavor. Plant them with the same herbs (mints, thyme, rosemary, sage, hyssop) as the garden varieties.

In garden intercropping, try not to put a plant that needs light where other, taller-growing plants will shade it, nor a moisture-loving plant with another that is greedy for water.

Just follow the general rules: asparagus with tomatoes; beans with carrots or summer savory; beet with onion or kohlrabi; members of the Cabbage family with aromatic plants or potatoes or celery; leeks with onions, celery, or carrots; turnips with peas.

Remember also the dislikes, and do not plant beans with onions, garlic, or gladiolus; beets with pole beans; the Cabbage family with strawberries, tomatoes, or pole beans; potatoes with pumpkin, squash, cucumber, sunflower, tomato, or raspberry.

Microclimate

A microclimate — a small area with special growing conditions — may result from an unusual natural feature on your land, such as a pond that moderates air temperatures. Or you can create a microclimate yourself by varying your plantings, adding a hedge, or covering a fence with vines. A hedge makes a permanent windbreak, but rows of tall corn will grow quickly and serve the same purpose for a season: to shade, protect, and limit air circulation for tender plants. So will vine plantings, such as grape, and also cucumbers (though these must be kept well watered during the summer, particularly if they take the western sun).

Mulch

Mulch can be almost anything that retards loss of moisture from the soil, but organic mulches, many of which also add nutrients, are considered the most helpful. These include chopped bark, buckwheat hulls, cocoa shells, coffee grounds, corncobs, cottonseed hulls, cranberry vines, evergreen boughs, grass clippings, hay, hops, leaves (particularly oak leaves, which repel slugs, cutworms, and grubs of June bugs), manure, peanut hulls, peat moss, pine needles (great to increase stem strength and flavor of strawberries), poultry litter, salt hay, sawdust, seaweed, stinging nettle, straw, sugarcane residue, tobacco stems, and wood chips and shavings. Particularly comprehensive information is found in *The Mulch Book* by Stu Campbell. (See Suggested Reading.)

Mulch, Sawdust

There is much to be said about a sawdust mulch, both for and against. Mulches like sawdust are particularly susceptible to spontaneous combustion, fresh sawdust can cause a depletion of soil nitrogen, and it is not good to use in summer because earthworms will avoid it.

On the good side, it is claimed by many authorities that blueberries mulched with sawdust will develop a larger, more fibrous root system and as an end result have a far higher yield. It is considered good mulch for raspberries and should be put on immediately after transplanting. Mixed with animal manures or poultry litter, it makes an acceptable mulch for many plants and shrubs where either one alone would not work well. Shavings or sawdust used for animal bedding makes an excellent mulch.

The type of tree from which the sawdust comes also has a bearing on the situation. Unweathered pine sawdust will decompose very slowly, so give it a bit of time to weather and turn gray before using. Sawdust from hardwood trees will rot much more rapidly than pine, spruce, or cedar, especially if weathered before using. Studies now show that the tannins and terpenes in sawdust that gardeners often fear really do little if any harm to the soil. (See *The Mulch Book* in Suggested Reading.)

pH

Experienced garden writers take it for granted that everybody knows what pH is all about. If you don't, relax; it isn't scary at all.

The pH of anything simply indicates its active acidity or alkalinity, expressed in units. The term is generally used in horticultural science to indicate a condition of the soil, and it's important to know, because many plants thrive only when the pH value of the soil closely approximates the optimum for their particular kind.

Soil acidity may be of two kinds, active and potential. It is a state in which the concentration of hydrogen ions (H^+) exceeds that of hydroxyl ions (OH^-). When you have an exact balance of H^+ and OH^- ions, you have neutrality. When the OH^- ions exceed the H^+ ions, you have alkalinity.

Active soil acidity represents the excess of H ions over the OH ions present in the soil solution. It is expressed in pH units on the pH scale. On this scale, 7 represents neutrality; higher readings indicate alkalinity and lower ones acidity. It is rare to find a soil with greater acidity than 3.5, or with greater alkalinity than 8.0. You should note, however, that the relationship between the figures is geometric. Acidity at pH 5 is ten times as great as at 6, and at pH 4, one hundred times.

What can you do about it if a soil test shows too much one way or the other? To neutralize acidity, the gardener adds lime, preferably the agricultural type. Gypsum or sulfur can be used to correct an alkaline condition. In my opinion all soils, but particularly alkaline ones, benefit from the use of compost or humus in the form of decomposed organic matter. A green manure crop plowed under also helps.

Shade

Shade is sometimes the decisive factor in companion planting. Nature does not arrange plants in long, straight rows, as we often do in our gardens. Try radishes in a foot-wide bed with no thinning. Put fast-growing lettuce such as 'Buttercrunch', 'Simpson', or 'Oakleaf' between cabbages, broccoli, Brussels sprouts, or even tomatoes, which will shade the young plants while they are growing. The lettuce will be up and out of the way when the slower-maturing plants need the room. You'll have a double crop on half the ground and with half the work, and you will also find that the taller plants give the lettuce just enough shade to keep it coming on crisp and sweet right into hot weather.

If you interplant early beets with late potatoes, the shade of the growing potatoes will benefit the beets, keeping them tender and succulent right into warm weather.

Plant melons between your onion rows, and by the time the onions are harvested the melons will be taking over the ground. While the vines are growing, the onions will protect them from insects.

After you harvest your early corn, let the stalks remain a while to shade a planting of fall cabbage, beans, peas, and turnips. When the fall garden is well established and the sun less warm, remove the cornstalks and use them for mulch right on the ground where they grew.

Many of the mints take kindly to shade and may be grown under trees. Sweet woodruff also likes shade and makes an excellent ground cover, while retaining moisture for other plants that give it protection from the sun. Tarragon and chervil like partial shade, too.

Succession Planting

This technique will enable you to make the most of a supply of compost or fertilizer. Heavy feeders such as broccoli, Brussels sprouts, cabbage, cauliflower, celeriac, celery, chard, cucumber, endive, kohlrabi, leek, lettuce, spinach, squash, sweet corn, and tomato should be planted in soil newly fertilized with well-decomposed manure.

Follow these heavy feeders with light feeders such as beet, carrot, radish, rutabaga, and turnip, which also like finely pulverized raw rocks and compost.

Legumes, the third group in succession planting, include broad and lima beans, bush and pole beans, peas, and soybeans. These soil improvers collect nitrogen on their roots and restore it to the soil.

Suicide in Plants

Why do most annual plants die in the autumn? It is possible that seeds inside mature fruits such as soybean pods send out hormones that cause plants to yellow and die even before nights cold enough for freezing cut them down.

Gardeners for years have known that if faded flowers are picked before they form seeds, the plants will continue to produce more flowers. Pansies are a good example. Among the vegetables, okra will continue from early spring to frost if the pods are kept picked before they harden.

This idea has been tested on soybeans. Growing pods were plucked from one side of the plant only and allowed to remain on the other. The side with the mature pods and seeds turned yellow and died, while the other remained healthy.

Two-Level Planting

Vegetables that occupy different soil strata often make good companions. Among these are asparagus with parsley and tomatoes, beets with kohlrabi, beets with onions, leeks with vine plants, garlic with tomatoes, carrots with peas, and also strawberries with bush beans.

Many combinations like this are possible, enabling the gardener with little space to virtually double the garden's yield, and at the same time improve the health and flavor of the vegetables planted together.

Do not put together plants that are competing for the same space and light, such as sunflowers and pole beans, or plants whose root excretions react unfavorably on each other, such as carrots and dill.

Two-Season Planting

Gardeners in areas that have a long growing season may find both a spring and fall garden possible. In the fall here in Oklahoma I can grow cauliflower, broccoli, Brussels sprouts, cabbage, collards, lettuce, radishes, and English peas, and they are practically insect-free. Some of the vegetables that require a long growing season to head up are a complete failure for me if planted in the spring, because of the hot midsummer conditions. I cannot give you exact dates; this has to be worked out by area according to where you live, but is well worth trying experimentally.

In many places, early-planted squash is more likely to withstand borers, which lay their eggs in July. Where I live, we have a rule: "Plant squash and cucumbers the first day of May before the sun comes up and they will be free of beetles." I find that fall-planted squash often escapes insects as well.

Radishes and cabbage may escape root maggots by careful timing. The Hessian fly's attacks on winter wheat may be avoided if the wheat is sown after the first week in October, when the fly is no longer active.

South Texas cotton farmers have found they can control the pink bollworm without insecticides by carefully establishing dead-line dates for both planting cotton and destroying the stalks after harvest.

Observe when insect infestations are worst on certain crops, and plant either earlier or later than you have in the past.

Vertical Gardening

If you have a fenced garden, here is an opportunity for both beauty and increased productiveness. Many plants take kindly to climbing. Cucumbers (such as Burpee 'Burpless') grow longer and straighter when trained on a fence. Scarlet runner beans climb rapidly and make a beautiful as well as a tasty display. I plant these with my chayotes, which bear good-tasting and attractive fruit in September.

Morning glories and pole beans do well together, and rambling roses are happy with gourds. When the roses are gone, the gourds will bear attractive blossoms and fruits without damage to the roses. If you grow the birdhouse type of gourd, these will be a bonus for your garden, dried and hung the following season to attract birds.

You might follow Oriental practice to relieve the somber dark green of pines by allowing clematis to grow into the trees, particularly the white-blooming type that forms huge panicles of scented flowers in late fall.

If you don't have a fence, try a tepee or wigwam made of four or more poles fastened together near the top and with soft wire or twine tied from pole to pole. The growing plants are trained to the poles by tying loosely. When they reach the top, pinch out the growing point of each plant, causing them to produce side shoots. This system is very good for vining squash. Soon the wigwam will be covered with a mass of attractive flowers, bright green leaves, and squashes.

Soil Improvement

Alfalfa *(Medicago sativa)*

This is one of the most powerful nitrogen-fixers of all legumes. A good stand can take 250 pounds of nitrogen per acre from the air each year. Alfalfa needs a deep soil without hardpan or an underlying rock layer, because it sends its roots down deep. Researchers have traced them for well over 100 feet, and 20 to 30 feet is average.

Alfalfa's deep-rooting ability is the source of its great nutritional power, feeding as it does from mineral-rich subsoil that has not been worn out and depleted. Alfalfa is strong in iron and is also a good source of phosphorus, potassium, magnesium, and trace minerals.

You can easily sprout alfalfa seeds in the kitchen, and you may even want to grow some in your garden for highly nutritious alfalfa greens, or use its leaves for tea. Alfalfa used as a meal is a great compost stimulant and activator, particularly good for composting household garbage.

Alfalfa will make good growth wherever dandelions grow. Dandelions themselves are deep divers, their presence indicating that the subsoil is easy to penetrate. Alfalfa grown in pastures will give protective shelter for shallower-rooting grasses, keeping other plants alive longer during spells of dry weather. As a trap crop, alfalfa will draw lygus bugs away from cotton. Two percent alfalfa provides sufficient control, but it should be planted about a month before the cotton.

Buckwheat *(Fagopyrum esculentum)*

Buckwheat is valuable as a soil builder and it will grow on very poor soils while collecting lots of calcium. Used in this manner it will take the light away from low-growing weeds, choking them out. If plowed under as green manure, it will sweeten the soil and make it more suitable for growing other crops. Buckwheat does not like winter wheat.

Calcium

Peas, beans, cabbages, and turnips revel in soil containing lime, but a few plants — notably those belonging to the Heath family, such as erica, azalea, and rhododendron — actually dislike it. Potatoes and a few cereals are not at their best if lime is applied to the ground immediately before they are planted or sown.

Land in need of lime does not respond to cultivation and manuring as it should, and often coarse weeds such as sheep sorrel flourish. Sometimes a green scum grows over the surface. A soil test that reveals excessive acidity indicates the need for liming.

Buckwheat accumulates calcium, and when composted or plowed under as green manure enriches the soil. Lupine *(Lupinus)* has roots that penetrate to surprising depths even on steep, gravelly banks or exposed sunny hills. It adds calcium to the soil, too, and is of value to grow on poor, sandy soils worthless for other purposes.

Scotch broom, a member of the Legume family, also accumulates calcium but may become a weed unless kept in check. Melon leaves are rich in calcium and should be added to the compost heap when the plants are spent.

Clover (Leguminosae)

Planting clover between rows of grapes will add nitrogen to the soil. This also works well in orchards or with companion grasses.

Clover dislikes henbane and also members of the Buttercup family, which secrete a substance in their roots that inhibits the growth of nitrogen bacteria and poisons the soil for clover. This poisoning is so effective that clover will disappear in a field if buttercups are increasing. Clover has a stimulating effect on the growth of black nightshade *(Solanum nigrum)*.

Compost

Compost is largely composed of decayed organic matter that has heated sufficiently to kill weed seeds and then has thoroughly decomposed. Plant preparations may be used to influence or speed up the fermentation process, and these — even when added in small amounts — can influence the entire operation. Once conditions are right, earthworms enter the compost pile and assist the other microorganisms in the breaking-down process.

Certain plants such as stinging nettle may be used to speed up or assist fermentation in the compost heap or manure pile. This plant is an excellent soil builder and, like comfrey, has a carbon-nitrogen ratio similar to barnyard manure. Nettles also contain iron.

Several other herbs are particularly well endowed with minerals and can be of value when incorporated into compost. These include dandelion, which absorbs between two and three times as much iron from the soil as other weeds; salad burnet, with its rich magnesium content; sheep sorrel, which takes up phosphorus; and chicory, goosegrass, and bulbous buttercup, which accumulate potassium. Horsetail shares honors with ribwort and bush vetch for a capacity to store cobalt. Thistles contain copper as a trace element.

Compost is the best fertilizer for herbs as well as garden vegetables and is particularly rich if weeds are put in the pile instead of being destroyed. Use all herb refuse obtained in the garden, too, and naturally all the kitchen waste, particularly in a household where cooking with herbs is a frequent feature.

Any organic material can be added, but refuse of a woody nature will decompose more rapidly if it is crushed or chopped first and used as a base mixed with materials such as grass clippings. Leaves picked up in the fall make good compost, but since they are apt to pack, they should be mixed with other material. Bulky materials form a solid mass of rotting vegetation, lack oxygen, and quickly become sour and greasy.

When making a pile, the site first should be well dug to allow for a quick entry of earthworms. Incorporate sods into the heap. Build your pile up to a height of about six feet with straight sides and a slightly concave top. The contents must be kept moist and allowed to heat so that weed seeds are killed. The quicker the heating, the earlier the heap should be turned and restacked.

Turpentine substance, washing from the leaves of conifers, will retard fermentation. Birch trees in the vicinity assist fermentation, even if their roots penetrate the heap. It is best, however, to have them at least six feet away.

Fertilizers, Nature's Own

We are all familiar with the ability of legumes to draw nitrogen from the air and "fix" it to their roots. Actually, there are many plants that get only about 5 percent of their nourishment directly from the soil.

Have you ever noticed how plants, particularly grass, look greener after a thunderstorm? This is not an optical illusion. They really *are* greener as a result of the electrically charged air, which frees its 78 percent nitrogen content in a water-soluble form.

Rain and lightning are fertilizing agents. Each time lightning strikes the earth, large amounts of nitrogen are charged into the ground. One authority states that 250,000 tons of natural nitrogen are produced every day in the 1,800 thunderstorms taking place somewhere on the earth. In some places this may amount to more than 100 pounds per acre per year. Rain also brings nitrogen — in some areas as much as 20 pounds per acre annually.

Sulfur comes down with the rain, possibly producing as much as 40 pounds per acre per year. Rainwater also contains carbonic acid, forming carbon dioxide in the soil where it is needed for the plant-feeding process. Millions of tons fall yearly, and when we consider that nearly half the makeup of a plant is carbon we realize how important this is. Evidence also seems to show that rare minerals such as selenium and molybdenum are washed down in rain.

Snow, which furnishes not only nitrogen but also phosphorus and other minerals, yields an extra bonus denied warm-climate areas. Snow contains 40 percent less heavy water, or deuterium oxide, than normal water. Deuterium is a heavy isotope, a form of hydrogen but a little different. Combined with water it does not form H_2O, the water molecule, but D_2O instead. Heavy water, according to the Russian scientists who observed this, slows down some chemical and biological processes of growing plants. When the heavy-water molecules are removed, plants seem to grow faster. Thus crops are aided in short-season, snowy climates such as that of Alaska. Even fog contributes to the soil's fertility, especially along the seacoast, where it brings in large quantities of iodine, nitrogen, and chlorine.

Dust, though sometimes disagreeable, has its good points too, containing minerals, organic matter, and beneficial organisms often in substantial quantities essential to plant growth. Dust may be carried for thousands of miles, even being held suspended for long periods in the upper atmosphere to be washed down eventually by rain. Many believe that dust is one of the most significant factors in restoring minerals to the exhausted soil and that it also contains bacteria important to healthy soil life.

Here's a way you can obtain some of the benefits of electro-culture without waiting for a thunderstorm. Tie your tomato plants to metal poles or trellises (ours are concrete-reinforcing wire bent in an inverted V-shape, with a row of tomato plants on each side), using nylon strips cut from discarded panty hose. These sturdy supports also attract static electricity. A friend who tried this reported that she harvested an abundant crop of extremely large tomatoes, and her plants continued producing right up to frost.

Green Manures

Green manures are cover crops, usually achieved by planting low-

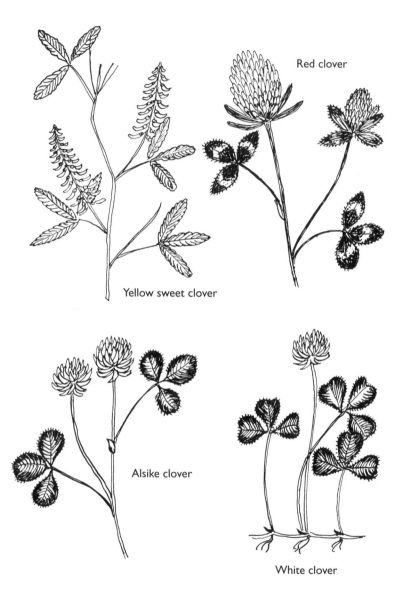

The clovers make fine green manure crops. Clover's growth is limited by Henbane and Buttercup family members.

priced seed. If fall-planted, the cover protects the soil surfaces of fields or garden plots from erosion from winter winds, snowstorms, and quick thaws. It acts as an insulating blanket, keeping the soil warmer in winter and cooler in summer. This encourages soil life activity in general and earthworms in particular. The more earthworms in the soil, the more channels they'll burrow deep in the subsoil, bringing to the surface useful minerals and nutrients that will increase the health and insect-resistance of food plants.

The roots of many green manure crops themselves reach deeply into the subsoil, where they absorb and bring up valuable nutrients. These revitalize the soil when the plants are plowed under to decompose.

Certain green manure crops, the legumes, have the ability to capture and fix large amounts of nitrogen from the air, also adding this important nutrient to the soil. Alfalfa is one of the best of these, and it is also high in terms of protein, which breaks down into usable nitrate fertilizer.

Other useful green manure cover crops are barley, bromegrass, buckwheat, cheat grass, alsike clover, cowpeas, lespedeza, millet, rape, spring rye, Italian ryegrass, winter rye, sorghum, soybeans, Sudan grass, sunflowers, common clovers, hairy vetch, and winter wheat.

For the home garden, kale makes a good, thick, nonleguminous green manure cover crop for the winter months. It is an easily grown, tasty food with a flavor that is improved by frost, and you can actually dig it out from under the snow in the dead of winter. When the kale starts growing again in the spring, it can be tilled under to add green manure to the soil for the spring garden.

Inoculants

Sold under various names such as Legume Aid (Burpee) and Nitragen (Farmer), these preparations are aids to peas, beans, soybeans, sweet peas, etc., for better blooms and increased yields. Treating legume seeds with the proper inoculants helps them to develop root nodules, which convert free nitrogen into plant food.

Legumes

Though nitrogen makes up 80 percent of the volume of the atmosphere, it is almost useless to most plants, for it must be changed into a compound before it can be used. Lightning combines or fixes small amounts of this nitrogen and oxygen in the air, thus forming oxides of nitrogen that are washed out of the atmosphere by rain or snow to reach the soil. (See *Fertilizers, Nature's Own* in this chapter.)

Nitrogen-fixing bacteria living in nodules on the roots of legumes — alfalfa, beans, clover, esparsette, kudzu, lespedeza, peas, peanuts, soybeans, winter (hairy) vetch, and others — can change atmospheric nitrogen into nitrogen compounds useful to themselves and other plants. Farmers for centuries have rotated their crops to take advantage of this increased soil fertility produced by legumes.

Clover is particularly beneficial if used as a green manure crop and plowed under before planting a crop of wheat or corn the following season. The decaying legume, rich in fixed nitrogen, increases the nitrogen content of the soil without the need for commercial fertilizers. A green manure crop of alfalfa will benefit a crop of cotton. Red clover may be used on soils too acid and too poorly aerated for alfalfa. The optimum pH for red clover is between 5.8 and 6.8 but it can stand a pH below 6.0 and still do reasonably well.

The steps in the nitrogen cycle can be traced in the growth and use of clover:

1. Atmospheric nitrogen is changed into proteins by the action of nitrogen-fixing bacteria growing in nodules on the clover roots.
2. After plowing under, the clover proteins are changed into ammonia by ammonifying bacteria.
3. Ammonia is then changed into nitrates by nitrifying bacteria.
4. Both ammonia and nitrates are used by other plants to form plant proteins.

The nitrogen-fixing bacteria of legumes benefit not only themselves but also other plants nearby. Peas and beans, for instance, benefit potatoes, carrots, cucumbers, cauliflower, cabbage, summer savory, turnips, radishes, corn, and most other herbs and vegetables.

Peanuts, another legume, can be used as a second crop after an earlier one is out, provided that you have a long growing season.

On larger acreages, lespedeza, kudzu, and esparsette may be used to aerate the soil and put nitrogen into it, while winter vetch and soybeans make excellent cover crops. Legumes sown with a small amount of mustard are helpful to grapevines and fruit trees. Peanuts are excellent to grow in an orchard of newly set nut trees.

Nitrogen-Fixing Plants
See *Legumes,* above.

Oats
See the chapter on Grasses, Grains, and Field Crops.

Potassium
Certain weeds indicate a soil rich in potassium. These are marsh mallow, knapweed, wormwood, opium poppy, fumitory, Russian thistle, tansy, and sunflower. Red clover, however, is a good indicator of potassium deficiency.

Tobacco takes up potassium in its leaves and stalks and is thus a good plant on the compost pile if it has not been sprayed with chemicals. Vegetables that like potassium are celeriac and leek.

Rhizobium
These are the bacteria that live in nodules on leguminous plants and turn atmospheric nitrogen into a useful form for building plant proteins. Unfortunately, they withhold their talents from such useful plants as corn and wheat. (See *Legumes* in this chapter.)

Saponin
Soapberry or chinaberry is the name of a group or genus of trees and shrubs that bear fruit containing a soapy substance called

saponin. Bouncing Bet is probably our best-known saponin-rich plant. Other unrelated plants such as primroses and carnations also have this quality, as well as many legumes, cyclamen tubers, camellia, viola, mints, horse chestnut, orach, pokeweed, runner beans, tomatoes, mullein, potatoes, and spinach. These plants are important because their decomposing remains create a favorable environment for the plants that come after them.

Commercial saponin is used as a foam producer in beverages and fire extinguishers and also as a detergent useful in washing delicate fabrics.

Seaweed

Kelp, a type of brown alga, provides fertilizer and is a source of the chemical element iodine, particularly the giant kelp of the Pacific. Chemists also extract from kelp large amounts of algin, which is useful in such commercial products as ice cream and salad dressings by virtue of its ability to hold several different liquids together.

Kelp is about 20 to 25 percent potassium chloride, and it also contains common salt, sodium carbonate, boron, iodine, and other trace elements. For gardeners who live on or near the seacoast, seaweeds are a natural and usually wasted resource that can be utilized for mulching and in compost piles. They are especially good materials to put around fruit trees. Another advantage is that decomposing seaweed is less attractive to mice than is straw.

Chopping seaweed may be advantageous if only for cosmetic reasons. It may be also advisable to rinse off the salt, but it is not necessary to be too fussy about this. The small amount left clinging will do no harm. Eelgrass, which dries into a light "hay" and doesn't pack down, is a perfect nonsmothering material for many plants. (See *Eelgrass* in the Wild Plants chapter.)

Another use for "sea power" to promote fertility is liquefied seaweed, which may be applied as a foliar fertilizer directly to the leaves of plants. It is particularly helpful to trees.

It has been found that seaweed as a fertilizer helps to promote frost resistance in tomatoes and citrus fruits, as well as increasing the sweetness of some fruits and giving better resistance to pests and diseases. Beets and parsnips respond badly to boron shortages in the soil, so chopped kelp makes an excellent mulch for them.

Seaweed helps to break down certain insoluble elements in the soil, making them available to plants. This quickens seed germination and further aids development of blossoms and fruits, resulting in increased yields.

For those who cannot readily obtain seaweed, there are seaweed preparations and fish emulsion, available at most garden centers and through gardening catalogs.

Another idea for gardeners who, like myself, live far inland is

Eelgrass makes an enriching mulch and is fine for composting.

to use water plants. Though not as rich in nutrients as seaweed, they make good mulch if chopped, and are good additions to the compost. Water hyacinth, a plant of tropical America, has escaped into the wild and has become a pest, choking many small streams. Dredged from waterways, it is valuable on the mulch pile. Here where I live, water lilies grow profusely in shallow pools and are easily obtainable. My husband, Carl, and I usually brought back a tubful of water weeds of some kind every time we went fishing.

Sweet Clover *(Melilotus alba* and *M. indica)*
This is not a true clover although it is a legume. White and yellow sweet clovers live for two years, and their large roots penetrate deeply into the soil. At the end of the second season, they decay to enrich the soil with nitrogen and decomposing vegetable material.

Sour clover, a kind of sweet clover used almost entirely to improve the soil, is often called melilot.

Spoiled sweet clover hay or poorly preserved silage never should be fed to animals. The hay contains coumarin, an anticoagulant, which develops toxicity as the clover decomposes and may cause both internal and external bleeding.

Weeds as Soil Builders
Many weeds seem to have a mysterious capacity for enriching soils. Jimsonweed (datura) grown near pumpkins will promote their health and vigor; the best watermelons come from the weediest part of the patch; onions grown with weeds (but not allowed to be overwhelmed) are apt to be larger than those in clean-cultivated rows.

This is particularly true if the weeds are the so-called "deep divers" that break up the subsoil, allowing the roots of the vegetable plants to have a larger-than-usual feeding zone. Deep divers sometimes bring up from below the hardpan mineral elements that the roots of food plants cannot reach. The high mineral content of weeds is another reason for adding them to the compost pile. (See *Compost* in this chapter.)

Pest Control

Bacillus thuringiensis (BT)

This is a selective bacterial disease, highly effective against caterpillars and the larvae of moths. During spore production, *Bacillus thuringiensis* produces crystals that act as a stomach poison on the insects eating the treated plants. This substance is not toxic to plants, man, or other animals, and can be applied even up to the day of harvest.

BT controls the fruit tree leaf roller, as well as tent caterpillars — the disease attacking the pest in the caterpillar stage after they have come out of the tent. The disease is widely used to protect commercial crops of celery, lettuce, cabbage, broccoli, cauliflower, mustard, kale, collards, and turnip greens. It is also effective against the tobacco budworm and the bollworm.

Special strains of BT have been developed to kill other pests such as mosquito larvae and Colorado potato beetles. BT products are widely available, under various brand names, from garden centers and mail-order catalogs.

Bean and Potato Combination

Bush beans planted with potatoes protect them against the Colorado potato beetle. In return, the potatoes protect the bush beans from the Mexican bean beetle. It is considered best to plant the beans and potatoes in alternate rows.

Birds

Birds around the garden are generally recognized as one of the best controls against insect pests. Particularly useful are the purple martins, which must catch flying insects almost constantly in order to live. Well-made martin houses set up away from large trees will attract martin colonies. Feeders and bird waterers will also encourage other birds to visit and nest near your garden.

Birds are particularly attracted to hackberry, chokecherry, elderberry, Tartarian honeysuckle, mulberry, dogwood, Japanese

The purple martins rid orchards and garden areas of incalculable numbers of injurious insects, devouring them in the winged stage.

barberry, red and black raspberries, viburnum, Hansen's bush cherry, Russian olive, hawthorn, and sunflowers. Evergreen trees and thornbushes are attractive for nest-building. Certain forms of cactus are attractive for this purpose in the Southwest.

Birds, however, can be too much of a good thing at times and may become very destructive to the food plants we grow for ourselves. From the Chinese we have this suggestion: When fruits start to ripen, hang sliced onions in the trees — the birds dislike the scent and will avoid the fruit. Hanging empty milk cartons in fruit trees from a string so they twirl in the breeze will deter many birds. Change their position occasionally, and perhaps also use bright, fluttering ribbons or strips of cloth.

If crows are a problem for a corn or watermelon patch, put up several stakes and string white twine around the patch, crisscrossing it through the center. To the birds this will look like a trap and they will avoid the patch.

Blackfly (Aphididae)

This insect is particularly detrimental to broad beans, and it is advisable to use a fermented extract of nettle to keep it under control. Its natural enemy, the lady beetle, will help. Intercropping with garlic, or placing an occasional plant of nasturtium, spearmint, or southernwood in the rows of beans, also is a good plan.

Borers

Nasturtiums planted around fruit trees repel borers, while garlic and other alliums such as onions and chives also are good.

Castor Bean *(Ricinus communis)*

Experiments have shown that castor beans planted around a garden will repel moles, and they also are good to repel mosquitoes.

This is an agricultural crop in some areas where it is grown for the oil in the seed, yet all parts of the plants are poisonous to livestock and humans, particularly the seed. Two or three seeds eaten by a child can be fatal and as few as six can cause the death of an adult. The beans also carry an allergen that causes severe reactions in some people when handling castor pomace. This danger can be eliminated if the seed heads are clipped off or destroyed before they mature.

Castor bean

To form an effective mole repellent, plant castor beans every five or six feet around the perimeter of the garden. Use them also as a companion crop: Plant several pole beans close to their bases and let them climb the tall-growing plants. The largest variety of castor bean, *zansibarensis,* grows eight feet tall, and has large leaves and beautiful variegated seeds of various colors. *Sanguineus* grows seven feet tall and 'Bronze King' five feet.

Cockroach *(Blatella)*
Extracts of chinaberry have been found useful against cockroaches and termites. The little-known cockroach plant *(Haplophyton cimicidum)* from Mexico also is valuable in controlling this pest.

Cutworm (Noctuidae)
A three-inch cardboard collar around young plants extended one inch into the ground and two inches above will foil cutworms. Use cardboard cut from toilet paper or paper towel rolls, or cut off the top and bottom from a quart-size milk carton and cut the remainder into three collars.

A used matchstick, toothpick, small twig, or nail set against the plant stem will keep the cutworm from wrapping itself around the plant and cutting it. Oak leaf mulch will repel cutworms, too.

Diatomaceous Earth
This effective remedy against many insects is made from the finely ground skeletons of small, fossilized, one-celled creatures called diatoms, which existed in the oceans and constructed tiny shells

about themselves out of the silica they extracted from the waters. The microscopic shells, deposited on the floor of the ancient seas, collected into deposits sometimes thousands of feet deep.

This earth contains microscopic needles of silica, which do their work by puncturing the bodies of insects, allowing vital moisture to escape from them. The insects die from dehydration. This earth is so finely milled that it poses no threat to either humans or animals, but these particles, when taken internally by insects, interfere with breathing, digestion, and reproductive processes.

Diatomaceous earth will not harm earthworms, which are structurally different from the insects. The earthworm's outside mucus protection, coupled with its unique digestive system, enables it to move through soil treated with diatomaceous earth without harm.

Many gardeners use diatomaceous earth as a dusting agent to give effective control against gypsy moths, codling moths, pink boll weevils, lygus bugs, twig borers, thrips, mites, earwigs, cockroaches, slugs, adult mosquitoes, snails, nematodes, all species of flies, corn worms, tomato hornworms, mildew, and so on. For field crops and in orchards, the diatomite particles are best applied with an electrostatic charger, which gives the particles a negative charge, causing them to stick to plant surfaces.

Eelworm

Eelworms or nematodes are tiny, sightless, eel-shaped organisms that pierce the roots of plants to feed or to lay their eggs inside, causing knots to form. When organic matter is incorporated into the soil, it encourages beneficial fungi and other nematodes that feed on the plant-parasitic variety of eelworms. These beneficial fungi grow in decomposing vegetable matter and kill the nematodes. It is possible to reduce wireworm and nematode attack, too, by placing a heavy dressing of barnyard manure on grassland before plowing.

These microscopic nuisances are discouraged by marigolds, scarlet sage *(Salvia),* or dahlias *(Dahlia).* Asparagus is a natural nematocide. Tomatoes grown near asparagus thus are protected, while in turn the tomatoes protect the asparagus from the asparagus beetle.

Flea Beetle *(Faltica* and *Epitrix)*
Flying insects such as flea beetles are known to dislike moisture. Very often they can be discouraged by watering the garden in full sunlight. I find them annoying but not particularly destructive to eggplant, tomato, turnip, and radish plants. The damage is mostly cosmetic, and strong plants quickly grow out of it, the plant becoming less attractive to the beetles as the leaves enlarge and toughen a little. Light cultivation and the addition of organic matter to the soil both discourage the beetles and help the plants.

Bruised elderberry leaves laid over the rows of plants are a deterrent to the beetles, and they also are repelled by mint and wormwood. Beetles attracted to radish or kohlrabi may be controlled by interplantings of lettuce.

Fumigation
Greenhouse gardeners, who frequently have difficulty controlling aphids, ants, and termites as well as that all-time pest, whitefly, find smoke from oak leaves effective. The leaves are not poisonous, do not kill soil bacteria, and leave no harmful residue. Smoke the leaves for about a half hour, keeping the greenhouse door tightly closed.

Garlic
See the Herbs chapter.

Gopher (Geomyidae)
These burrowing rodents may be repelled by plantings of scilla bulbs. The scillas, sometimes called squills, are flowering, bulblike ornamentals that have grasslike leaves and clusters of flowers at the top of long stems. They are easy to grow, and bloom in the early spring. They may be grown among vegetables as well as in flower beds. But be cautious — the bulbs should never be eaten.

Grasshopper (Tettigoniidae and Locustidae)

Grasshoppers are very difficult to control, especially where they come in from surrounding fields, but this spray will help: Grind together two to four hot peppers, one mild green pepper, and one small onion, and add to one quart water. Let stand 24 hours and strain. This mixture also is good against aphids.

During times of grasshopper infestation, an after-harvest plowing will discourage egg-laying, while spring tilling before seeding will prevent grasshoppers from emerging from the eggs still present. Extracts of chinaberry have proved useful, while sabadilla dust or extract is effective against these and many other insects. (See *Insecticides, Botanical* in this chapter.)

Grasshoppers can be attracted by this bait: Fill several two-quart mason jars with a 10 percent molasses solution and place around the area where the infestation is the worst.

Chickens are of great value in an orchard, for they eat grasshoppers and other insects and at the same time add their manure to aid the fertility of the soil. The coop may be moved every few days to a new location.

Wild birds attracted to the garden eat a great many grasshoppers and surprisingly cats will kill and eat them, too. I think this is partly for the fun they get out of the chase.

Grasshoppers will eat almost anything except horehound, but grasshopper-resistant varieties of corn and wheat have been developed.

Ichneumonid Wasp *(Campoletis perdistinctus)*

This wasp has been found by the Brownsville Experiment Station in Texas to parasitize at least 27 destructive species of moths and butterflies, but it *prefers* to deposit its eggs in bollworms and tobacco budworms.

Insect Attractants, Botanical

Insects are largely attracted by scent and may be lured away from certain crops by other plants placed nearby. Plants such as nasturtium and mustard, both of which contain mustard oil, frequently are used for this purpose. These are called trap crops. Insects feed on and lay their eggs in trap crops, which should be destroyed before the eggs hatch.

Insect Repellents, Botanical

Insect repellents may be prepared from crushed leaves, infusions, or essential oils of such botanicals as citronella, eucalyptus, pennyroyal, bergamot, cedarwood, clove, rose geranium, thyme, wintergreen, lavender, cassia, anise, sassafras, bay laurel, and pine tar. Ginkgo, elder, pyrethrum, and lavender repel ticks or other insects. Other plants such as cedar, quassia, and teakwood themselves are immune to insects.

See also the Insect Control through Companion Planting chart, page 154, in this chapter.

Insecticides, Botanical

Several plant derivatives are available commercially as insecticides. (See Sources.) These materials break down more quickly than man-made insecticides and (except for nicotine) are relatively non-toxic to humans when used as directed. They kill bees and other beneficial insects as well as pests, however, and can be toxic to other life-forms such as fish. As with any pest-control products, read the label and follow the directions exactly.

Pyrethrum is prepared from the flowers of *Chrysanthemum cinerariafolium* or *C. roseum.* It is used alone or in combination with other botanicals against a wide variety of pests, including aphids, leafhoppers, spider mites, harlequin bugs, and imported cabbageworms.

Rotenone comes from the roots of tropical plants and is a powerful stomach poison for chewing insects.

Nicotine. Tobacco and its main alkaloid, nicotine, have been used as an insecticide since the late seventeenth century. Nicotine, a contact poison, is toxic to mammals as well as insects and should be handled very carefully.

Ryania, from a Latin American shrub native to Trinidad, does not always kill insects outright but rather makes them ill, causing them to stop feeding.

Sabadilla. When heated or treated with an alkali, the seeds of this plant become toxic to many insects. Oddly enough, this quality increases with age during storage. The extract is effective against a large group of insects such as grasshoppers, corn borers, codling moths, webworms, aphids, cabbage loopers, and squash bugs. Be cautious in handling the dust and do not breathe it in.

Neem oil is made from the seeds of the neem tree, native to India. It is useful against Japanese beetles and the adults of many other chewing insects, acting as a repellent and as an appetite suppressant, and also stops the development of larvae.

Insect-Resistant Vegetables and Grains

Every garden has both "good" and "bad" bugs, yet from a gardener's point of view only a few are relatively destructive. Some vegetables seem to have a natural, built-in resistance: carrots, beets, endive (including escarole and witloof chicory), chives, okra, Egyptian onions, parsley, peppers, and rhubarb. Under good growing conditions, lettuce might be added to this list, too.

Numerous vegetables and herbs listed in this book help other vegetables to resist insects when grown with or near them. Scientists have done a great deal of research, also, on why certain other plants are attractive to insects. They have come up with something that organic gardeners knew all along: Insects prefer to eat plants having high concentrations of free amino acids, such concentrations being enhanced if the plants are improperly nourished. Organically grown vegetables produced on balanced, healthy soils have significantly lower levels of free amino acids in their tissues than plants grown where chemical fertilizers have destroyed the balance. Such "organic" vegetables are less tasty to insects.

In addition, vegetable varieties have been bred for resistance to specific pests. Your county's Cooperative Extension Service may have recommendations on good choices for local conditions.

INSECT CONTROL THROUGH COMPANION PLANTING

Legumes planted in a rotation will protect grain crops and grasses from white grubs and corn rootworm. Chinch bug on corn and flea beetles are controlled by growing soybeans to shade the bases of the plants. The herbs in this chart may be planted as specific controls.

HERB	DETERS
Basil	Flies and mosquitoes
Borage	Tomato worms
Castor bean	Moles and plant lice
Catnip	Flea beetles
Datura	Japanese beetles
Dead nettle	Potato bugs
Flax	Potato bugs
Garlic	Japanese beetles, aphids, weevils, fruit tree borers, spider mites
Henbit	General insect repellent
Horseradish	Potato bugs (plant at corners of plot)
Hyssop	Cabbage moths
Lavender	Clothes moths (dry and place in garments)
Marigold	Mexican bean beetles, nematodes, and many other insects
Mint	White cabbage moths, dried against clothes moths
Mole plant	Moles and mice (mole plant is a species of euphorbia)
Nasturtium	Aphids, squash bugs, striped pumpkin beetles, woolly aphids
Pennyroyal	Ants and plant lice
Peppermint	White cabbage butterflies, ants
Petunia	Beetles

Herb	Deters
Pot marigold	Asparagus beetles, tomato worms, and many other insects
Rose geranium	Oil or crushed leaves as insect repellents
Rosemary	Cabbage moths, bean beetles, carrot flies, and malaria mosquitoes
Rue	Japanese beetles
Sage	Cabbage moths, carrot flies, ticks
Santolina	Moths
Sassafras	Plant lice
Southernwood	Cabbage moths, malaria mosquitoes
Spearmint	Ants, aphids
Stinging nettle	Aphids, blackflies
Summer savory	Bean beetles
Tansy	Flying insects, Japanese beetles, striped cucumber beetles, squash bugs, and ants
Thyme	Cabbageworms
White geranium	Japanese beetles
Wormwood	Animal intruders, cabbageworm butterflies, black flea beetles, malaria mosquitoes

Ladybugs

These famous eaters of aphids may be purchased for garden release. (See Sources.) The problem, especially in small gardens, is to keep them there. If there is a real need for their services and there is plenty of ladybug food around, they are more likely to stay.

The way you release them will make a difference. Do not strew them about like grains of corn but rather place them by handfuls — carefully — around the base of infested plants. Their natural instinct is to climb the nearest plant and start hunting for food. Do your "seeding" gently, since rough handling, especially in warm weather, may excite them to flight. Early morning or evening is the best time.

Lamb's-quarters, which sometimes harbor the leaf miner, also may play host to the beneficial ladybug. Newly placed ladybugs are dependent on their hosts (which also may be Chinese celery, cabbage, or other plants), and they must find aphids in sufficient quantity to keep them in the vicinity and ensure reproduction. After one mating a female will produce from 200 to 1,000 offspring.

In the spring you can often find the eggs of ladybugs on the undersides of leaves, near their early food supply, aphids. You will see them standing on end in clusters of 5 to 50, generally yellow or orange in color. The alligator-shaped larvae are blue-black and orange-spotted.

Mice

Mice and rats are repelled by fresh or dried leaves and the oils of mints, by camphor, and by pitch pine. Mothballs repel rabbits as well as mice but should not be used where food crops are grown or where children can pick them up.

Sea onions, white lavender, wormwood, and spurge repel mice, while everlasting pea is useful against field mice, and leaves of dwarf elder protect against mice in granaries.

If mice like your garden too much, repel them with bulb plantings of daffodil, narcissus, scilla, or grape hyacinth.

Milk

Cows and goats give more and richer milk when fed on stinging nettle hay or members of the Umbelliferae family. We always saved discarded carrots and carrot tops when we kept milk goats, which also liked prunings from rosebushes if the thorns were not too prominent.

Skim milk may be used as a spray on tobacco and other plants subject to mosaic virus, and on peppers and tomatoes grown in the greenhouse. Pickers in commercial pepper and tomato plots find it useful to dip their hands in skim milk to avoid transmitting the mosaic virus, while whey proteins are effective, too.

A milk and blood spray has been used in orchards to control fungi, and a milk and coal tar mixture against chinch bug.

Sour milk or butttermilk may be sprinkled over cabbages against cabbageworms.

Milky Spore Disease *(Bacillus popillae)*

This widely used bacterial organism gives protection against the Japanese beetle by producing a fatal disease in the grub. Because it brings about an abnormal white coloring in the insect, it is called milky.

It was developed in 1933 when a field survey in central New Jersey discoverd a few abnormally white Japanese beetle grubs, which examination showed were teeming with bacterial spore.

This disease was studied by the Bureau of Entomology and Plant Quarantine, where attempts were made to culture it for release. Treatment with the milky spore on experimental plots showed a more than 90 percent mortality in two months. In areas where the disease had been established naturally, equally high kills were found. This disease, occurring naturally in Japan, has kept the beetle from becoming a serious problem there.

The spore ordinarily needs only one application and then continues and spreads itself. It can be applied to the soil at any time except on a windy day or when the ground is frozen, but it is best to treat mowed or cropped areas. Apply a teaspoonful of the spore disease powder on grass or sod spots three to four feet apart and in rows the same distance apart. The beetle grub feeding in the soil will then take in the bacteria spores.

When a healthy grub becomes infected, the spores give rise to slender vegetative rods, which multiply in the blood by repeated divisions. In a short time the normally translucent blood of the grub will become milky in appearance, and eventually the grub dies. The spores stored in the body cavity then are released in the soil and are taken up by other grubs that in turn become infected. As the cycle continues, the spores increase in number and, since more grubs are killed, fewer and fewer adult beetles emerge to feed on crops. The disease is cumulative and self-perpetuating.

Milky spore disease is sold under several trade names. (See Sources.)

Neem oil is being increasingly used as a Japanese beetle control with considerable success. (See *Insecticides, Botanical* in this chapter.)

Less effective but still useful methods of combating the Japanese beetle include companion plantings of geraniums among roses and grapes to drive the beetles away. Larkspur eaten by the beetles will kill them, while soybeans work as a trap crop. The

beetles are rarely destructive to cabbage, carrots, cauliflower, eggplant, onions, lettuce, parsley, peas, potatoes, radishes, spinach,
squash, sweet potatoes, tomatoes, and turnips.

Molasses Grass *(Mellimus minutiflora)*

This is one of nature's very own insect traps. The covering of glan-
dular hairs exudes a viscous oil capable of trapping small pests such
as ticks. It does not kill them, but stops them from crawling
upward to come in contact with an animal. Cattle pastured on this
grass in Guatemala were found to be free of ticks within a year,
and it has been planted in Florida with good results. At the same
time it provides good forage for cattle, which like to graze on it. It
also repels mosquitoes and the tsetse fly.

Moles (Gryllidae)

Moles generally are considered a nuisance, and they do consume
beneficial creatures such as earthworms, but they also feed on
Japanese beetle grubs. They are deterred by a few plants of caper
spurge *(Euphorbia lathyrus)* strategically placed, by daffodil bulbs,
and by castor bean plants. Thorny twigs of raspberry, rose,
hawthorn, or mesquite pushed into burrows will scratch the moles
and cause them to bleed to death.

Mosquitoes

Garlic-based oil (see *Garlic* in the Herbs chapter) is effective in
killing mosquito larvae in ponds. Myristicin, a synthesized compound found in parsnips, also is effective as a selective insecticide
against the larvae, as is *Bacillus thuringiensis.*

The leaves of molasses grass *(Mellimus minutiflora)* and sassafras are mosquito repellents, and I find that castor beans planted
around my garden make it more pleasant to work there in the
long, cool western twilights when I do most of my garden work.

Euell Gibbons says that American pennyroyal *(Hedeoma pule-
gioides)*, sometimes called squaw mint and a native American plant
not to be confused with the European pennyroyal *(Mentha
pulegium)*, is a natural insect repellent. A handful crushed and

rubbed on the skin will not only emit a pleasant smell but also repel mosquitoes and gnats.

Moths and Millers

If moths and millers are troublesome in fruit trees, place one cup molasses in one and a half cups water and hang in small buckets or cans from the limbs. Remove the insects occasionally or make new solutions. This remedy is particularly helpful if used in peach trees.

Nematodes

See *Eelworms* in this chapter.

Oil Sprays

Used properly and at the right time, dormant oil sprays are effective, particularly in orchards, against many chewing and sucking insects. The oils make a tight film over insect eggs, causing suffocation.

Apply heavy dormant oil sprays only in early spring over leafless trees. However, lighter, more refined oils have been developed in recent years and can be used at other stages of growth.

Pepper, Hot *(Capsicum frutescens,* var. *fasciculatum* and var. *longum)*

Hot red peppers are among the most useful plants in the garden as well as the most flavorsome.

Grind hot peppers and mix with water and a little powdered real soap to make an infusion for spraying plants infested with aphids. Dry cayenne pepper may be dusted on tomato plants attacked by caterpillars.

However, if you note long green hornworms on tomatoes, do not be too quick to spray. Watch to see if any of the tiny parasitic wasps that build noticeable white cocoons all over tomato hornworms are present. Do not harm these predators with sprays — they may be doing your work for you.

Ground red peppers placed around eggplants and rubbed on the leaves will help repel eggplant pests, and the dried pods, pulverized and sprinkled on corn silk, will give protection against raccoons.

Another all-purpose spray may be made of ground pepper pods, onions, and a bulb of garlic. Cover this mash with water, let stand 24 hours, and strain. Add enough water to make a gallon of spray. Use several times daily on roses, azaleas, chrysanthemums, or beans to hold down serious infestations. Do not throw away the mash, but bury the residue among the plants where insects occur.

Protect your hands with gloves when you work with hot peppers, and be very careful not to get the juice in your eyes.

Praying Mantis (Mantidae)

Despite its ferocious appearance, this is one of our most beneficial insects, and it will not harm any vegetation in the garden, dining only on other insects. When young it eats the soft-bodied insects, the cutting and sucking aphids and leafhoppers; when fully mature it kills and eats chinch bugs, crickets, locusts, bees, wasps, beetles, flies, spiders, tent caterpillars, and many others.

Though mantids usually are found in warm countries, the common European mantid can live in the northern United States. A full-grown large mantid varies from two to five inches in length depending on the kind, yet it will easily escape notice because in form and color it closely resembles the plants on which it rests.

Female mantids lay their eggs in masses, gluing them to trees and shrubs with a sticky substance from their bodies. The eggs remain there all winter, and if you carefully examine thorny

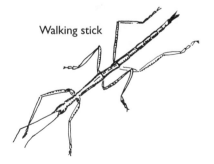

Walking stick

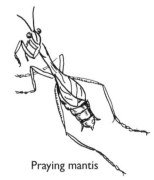

Praying mantis

bushes, brush, hedges, and berry bushes in autumn after leaves have fallen, you may find the hardened froth mass egg cases. You can collect some from marshes and waste areas for your own garden, but never strip the area clean.

To place them properly, allow one egg case for each major shrub or about four for each quarter acre (without shrubbery). Select a sheltered spot and tie or tape the cases securely about two to four feet above the ground.

Early in the spring the mantis will start to aid you, emerging in bright sunshine usually from early May to late June, just at the time when a large variety of insect fare is likely to be available.

Each creature is fastened to the egg by a tenuous cord that it must break. After doing so it will drop and then climb to surrounding foliage. Mantids are poor flyers and slow movers and usually remain in the area as long as they continue to find food. And once introduced, they are likely to multiply and extend control. Though many of the young may not live, still enough survive to perpetuate themselves. You can obtain mantid egg cases commercially through the mail, usually between November and early May. (See Sources.)

Rabbit *(Oryctolagus cuniculus)*

Onions are repellent to rabbits and may be interplanted with cabbage and lettuce. An old garden hose cut in lengths of a few feet each and arranged to look like snakes will frighten rabbits away.

Animal fat can be painted on young fruit trees, and a thin line of dried blood or blood meal sprinkled around the garden often acts as a repellent. Try a dusting of aloes on young plants, or shake wood ashes, ground limestone, or cayenne peppers on plants while they are wet with dew.

Raccoon *(Procyon lotor)*

Farmers have been planting pumpkins and corn together for centuries to discourage raccoons. Put the pumpkin seeds about four feet apart. As the corn approaches maturity, the big, wide pumpkin leaves will grow around the stalks. It is believed that the coons

Repellents for the corn-loving raccoon include nearby cucumber, melon, pumpkin, or squash vines. Red or black pepper on the corn silk also may help.

will not come into the corn rows because they like to be able to stand up and look around while they eat, and the big leaves make that impossible.

Other methods to control raccoons include sprinkling black or red pepper on the corn silks. This does not affect the taste of the corn.

For a small planting, a wire "corn cage" or an electric fence is sure protection. If a six- or twelve-volt battery is used, the fence will be harmless. It need be turned on only at night, since raccoons sleep during the day. Another solution is to use a small transistor radio (enclosed in a plastic bag to protect it from rain or dew), placing it in the patch at ripening time. Turn it on at night.

Root Knot

If the fresh tops of asparagus are crushed and steeped in water, the solution may offer protection to vegetables where root knot, stubby root, and meadow nematodes are suspected. Marigolds are also useful against meadow nematodes. (See *Eelworms* in this chapter.)

Root Maggot

Root maggots may be repelled by a mulch of oak leaves.

Salt, Common (Sodium chloride)

Salt has a damaging effect on most plants and should not be used except where the soil is to be rested for a time afterward. It is useful to kill Canada thistle or quack grass and will give best results if put on after the weeds are freshly cut. Apply several times, taking care to do so only in dry weather. Salt put on slugs will dissolve them.

Slugs and Snails (*Agriolimax campestris* and Helicidae)

These beasties cause most of their damage at night in places where the ground is damp. They are topers: They love beer and will

The skunk's protection, butyl mercaptan, can be neutralized with tomato juice. Skunks have some benefit in keeping large insects and mice in check.

drown in saucers of it. Even empty beer cans placed in the garden attract them by their odor. They also love honey and will drown in saucers of that. What a way to go!

Since ordinary table salt will dissolve slugs, I find it handy to carry a small salt shaker in my pocket to use when I spot them. I feel no compunction, for these slimy creatures will destroy my choicest cabbage and lettuce heads if they get a chance.

Tobacco stem meal discourages slugs, and white hellebore controls them on grapes and cherries. They dislike tanbark or oak leaves, and wormwood will repel them by its bitterness. Snails are reluctant to cross lines of ashes or hydrated lime.

Soap

In using most sprays made from botanicals it is a good idea to add a small amount of real soap to help the materials adhere. Washing plants down with just plain soapy water is an excellent practice in many instances, for soap appears to have antiseptic qualities useful against many plant diseases. Insecticidal soaps, which can be useful against a variety of insects, are available from garden centers and by mail order (see Sources).

Spider *(Arachnida)*

Some mites and spiders are natural predators, our valuable allies that dine on many destructive insects. One type of predaceous mite is used to control plant-feeding insects on avocado and citrus crops.

Spider Mite *(Acarina)*

Spider mites, also called red spiders, are apt to show up suddenly in hot weather. They sometimes can be removed from plants by spraying

The garden spider is one of the best helpers to the vegetable grower.

forcibly with a stream of plain water, and once dislodged from a plant they seldom return. A 3 percent oil spray, pyrethrum dust, or a spray of onions and hot peppers may be used, and I have found that garlic will repel the mites on tomato plants, while ladybugs are their natural enemies.

Tea Leaves

Mix tea leaves with radish and carrot seed to prevent maggots.

Termite (Termitidae)

Since most termites cannot live without water, cutting off the source of moisture usually kills them. Silica aerogel is effective, and extracts of chinaberry will kill about 98 percent of them.

Toad *(Bufo)*

Both toads and frogs consume many insects, one toad being able to eat up to 10,000 insects in three months' time — and many of these will be cutworms. Other pests eaten by toads include crickets, grubs, rose chafers, rose beetles, caterpillars, ants, squash

Horned toads, like true toads, are great friends of the gardener, devouring great numbers of insects. Help them find shelter in your garden area.

bugs, sow (pill) bugs, potato beetles, moths, mosquitoes, flies, slugs, and even moles.

Toads do *not* cause warts and are not poisonous to man, though they exude a slime distasteful to their enemies. If you want to secure some toads for your garden, look around the edges of swamps and ponds in spring. Once secured, they need shelter. A clay flowerpot with a small hole broken out of the side will serve for housing if buried a few inches in the ground in a shady place. They also need a shallow pan of water and, if your garden is not fenced, protection from dogs and other creatures.

In the Southwest, we use the horned toads (really lizards) in the same way. They can withstand more heat and thrive in my garden, apparently living on dew and insects. They bury themselves in the ground during winter, emerging when the weather warms up.

Tobacco
See *Nicotine* under *Insecticides, Botanical,* in this chapter.

Trap Crops
See *Insect Attractants, Botanical,* in this chapter.

Whitefly *(Trialeurodes vaporariorum)*
Whitefly is one of the insects known to thrive on certain shortages of minerals in the soil, and experiments have shown that greenhouse whiteflies attack tomatoes only when phosphorus or magnesium is deficient.

Botanical controls include nasturtium, particularly good to grow in greenhouses with tomatoes. Oak leaves burned in a greenhouse for a half-hour period are helpful, and nicotine may be used as a spray.

Whitefly can be controlled biologically by a small parasite called *Encorsia formosa* (see Sources). Ladybugs also are a control, as are aphis lions (the larvae of lacewing flies).

White Hellebore *(Veratrum album)*

White hellebore is a member of the Lily family whose roots and rhizomes contain insecticidal substances. It becomes less toxic upon exposure to light and air and has little residual effect, making it less poisonous to use than more persistent materials.

The use of white hellebore is centuries old. The Greeks mixed it with milk to kill flies, and it was a favorite remedy of the Romans against mice and rats. Today it is used to control many leaf-eating insects such as sawflies, which attack ripening fruit, and also for slugs and cabbageworms.

Wood Ashes

Wood ashes sprinkled around the base of cauliflower and onion plants are a popular remedy to control maggots. They are also used against clubroot, red spider, bean beetles, and scab on beets and turnips, as well as aphids on peas and lettuce. They are good, too, around such plants as corn, which need to develop strong stalks.

A thin paste made of wood ashes and water and painted on the trunks is used to control tree borers. A handful each of wood ashes and hydrated lime, diluted with two gallons of water, makes a spray for the upper and lower sides of cucurbit leaves to control cucumber beetles.

Woodchuck *(Marmota monax)*

If woodchucks are a problem, spray the plants they are nibbling with a solution of water and hot pepper.

Poisonous Plants

Humans perhaps were given dominion over the birds and beasts and the lilies of the field (including thorn apple and castor bean) because they have (or should have) the ability to distinguish the good from the bad.

Since the beginning of time, people the world over have lived close to hundreds of plants that can cause irritation, illness, or even death. A few are seriously poisonous; a far greater number are moderately so, producing varying degrees of illness or irritation. Some cause dermatitis, hay fever, or other illnesses as a result of the allergic sensitivity rather than the direct toxicity of the plant.

It would be virtually impossible to ban every plant that is inedible, drug-producing, or even irritating to the skin. Moreover, many such plants are the source of valuable medicines or serve us well as natural insecticides when wisely and carefully used in our gardens.

Children should be taught which plants are harmful and which may be used or eaten or touched with safety. Caution the child old enough to understand about eating wild berries, fruits, and nuts or chewing on bark, branches, or stems. Watch younger children just as you keep them from running into the street or keep dangerous household preparations out of reach. For poisonous plants, whether present in your own garden or in fields nearby, *will* be encountered.

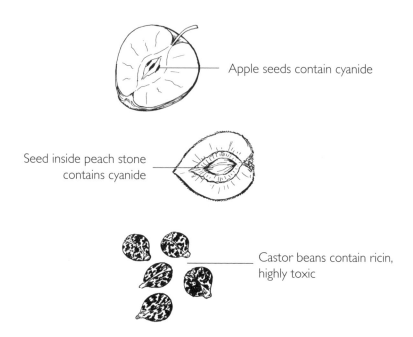

Apple seeds contain cyanide

Seed inside peach stone
contains cyanide

Castor beans contain ricin,
highly toxic

Apples, peaches, and castor beans contain highly poisonous parts.

Dozens of these plants are attractive garden flowers or shrubs, greatly prized for their beauty or usefulness in landscaping, so many adults and most children do not realize their poisonous characteristics. Who would think, for instance, that daffodils are dangerous? Nevertheless, the bulbs can be fatal if eaten. The beautifully marked castor beans are a natural plaything for a small child, and little children often put things into their mouths. Yet for this poison there is no available antidote.

Even older children have been known to try the "nuts" inside a peach stone. How do I know? Because as a child I tried one of these seeds. They resemble almonds, which I dearly loved. I didn't know that they contain cyanic acid and that a few of them could kill me. Fortunately, the bitter flavor stopped me after the first bite. Parents can't think of everything to tell children not to do, so it is indeed fortunate that many dangerous plants do have an unpleasant taste.

But if my mother didn't know about the peach stones (and I kept my experiment a secret), there wasn't much else she didn't know about. She was a skilled herbalist, and I grew up with the salves and tonics she prepared and brewed from the plants she gathered.

She often told me of her adventures in the Indiana woods where she went to gather ginseng. Later, when she and my father were married, she transferred her herb-gathering activities to Kentucky, and still later, when the family came out to Oklahoma, then Indian territory, she found literally new fields to conquer. She learned much herbal lore from Native Americans, who gave her the name Hill-lea-tah-ha, meaning "one-who-thinks-good." In those days when there were few doctors and most people made their own medicines, her knowledge was greatly respected. And she was fortunate to be completely unaffected by poison ivy, an immunity that I too am happy to have.

To this day I still grow many of the plants my mother brought in from the woodland to use for their therapeutic or insecticidal properties. Until recently I did not think of them as "companion plants," though I was clearly aware of their effect when grown in proximity to flowers, fruits, and vegetables.

While I have known since childhood most of the plants likely to be encountered in garden or woodland, there are many things about plants that I am still learning — for instance, that some nonpoisonous plants have been contaminated by neighboring poisonous ones through a chemical chain. The poisonous plant absorbs selenium from the soil, something the "innocent" plants cannot do. In dying and decomposing, the poisonous plant leaves the selenium in a changed state, in a sense predigested, which causes the harmless plant during its next season's growth to draw the toxic substance into its own system.

I have no degree in botany, nor am I an expert on poisonous plants. Neither shall I try to cover *all* of them in this brief chapter. Excellent books are available for those who are interested in pursuing the subject in greater detail. Here are only those plants that are most likely to be found in flower or vegetable gardens, or that may arrive, blown in by the wind or other means, as weeds. I have noted with a "D" those plants likely to cause dermatitis, a susceptibility that of course varies from person to person.

POISONOUS PLANTS

SCIENTIFIC NAME	COMMON NAME	POISONOUS PART OF PLANT
Abrus precatorius	Rosary pea	One rosary pea seed causes death
Acokanthera spp.	Bushman's poison	All parts very poisonous
Aconitum spp.	Monkshood	All parts, especially roots and seeds, very poisonous; characterized by digestive upset and nervous excitement
Adonis aestivalis	Summer adonis	Leaves and stem
Aesculus spp.	Horse chestnut, buckeye	Leaves and fruit
Ailanthus altissima	Tree of heaven	Leaves, flowers; D
Amaryllis belladonna	Belladonna lily	Bulbs
Anemone patens	Pasqueflower	Young plants and flowers
Arisaema triphyllum	Jack-in-the-pulpit	All parts, especially roots (like dumb cane), contain small, needlelike crystals of calcium oxalate that cause intense irritation and burning of the mouth and tongue
Asclepias spp.	Milkweed	Leaves and stems
Asparagus officinalis	Asparagus	Spears contain mercaptan, which may cause kidney irritation if eaten in large amounts; young stems; D
Baileya multiradiata	Desert marigold	Whole plant
Brunsvigia rosea	Garden amaryllis, naked lady	Bulbs
Buxus sempervirens	Common box	Leaves; D
Calonyction spp.	Moonflower	Seeds

Scientific Name	Common Name	Poisonous Part of Plant
Cephalanthus occidentalis	Buttonbush	Leaves
Cestrum spp.	Cestrum, night-blooming jessamine	Leafy shoots
Cicuta	Water hemlock	All parts fatal, causing violent and painful convulsions
Clematis vitalba	Traveler's joy	Leaves
Colchicum autumnale	Autumn crocus, meadow saffron	Leaves are very poisonous
Conium maculatus	Poison hemlock	All parts
Convallaria majalis	Lily of the valley	Leaves and flowers very poisonous
Corynocarpus laevigata	Karaka nut	Seeds
Crinum asiaticum	Crinum lily	Bulbs
Crotalaria spp.	Canary bird bush	Seeds

The handsome lily of the valley has poisons in both leaves and flowers.

SCIENTIFIC NAME	COMMON NAME	POISONOUS PART OF PLANT
Cypripedium spp.	Lady's slipper orchid	Hairy stems and leaves; D
Cytisus laburnum (see Laburnum)		
Daphne spp.	Daphne	Bark, leaves and fruit fatal; a few berries can kill a child
Datura spp.	Angel's trumpet, thorn apple, jimsonweed	All parts cause abnormal thirst, distorted sight, delirum, incoherence, and coma; has proved fatal
Delphinium spp.	Larkspur, delphinium	Young plants and seeds cause digestive upset; may be fatal
Dicentra spp.	Dutchman's-breeches, bleeding heart	Leaves and tubers may be poisonous in large amounts; fatal to cattle
Dieffenbachia seguine	Dumb cane	Stems and leaves cause intense burning and irritation of mouth and tongue; death can occur if base of tongue swells enough to block the throat

The digitalis in foxglove is a powerful heart stimulant. It may be fatal if the leaves are eaten.

Scientific Name	Common Name	Poisonous Part of Plant
Digitalis purpurea	Foxglove	Leaves cause digestive upset and mental confusion; may be fatal in large amounts
Duranta repens	Golden dewdrop	Fruits and leaves
Echium vulgare	Blue weed	Leaves and stems; D
Euonymus europaea	European burning bush	Leaves and fruit
Eupatorium rugosum	White snakeroot	Leaves and stems
Euphorbia spp.	Euphorbia, snow-on-the-mountain, poinsettia	Milky sap; D
Ficus spp.	Fig	Milky sap; D
Fragaria spp.	Strawberry	Fruit; D
Gelsemium sempervirens	Yellow jessamine	Flowers and leaves; roots; D
Ginkgo biloba	Ginkgo, maidenhair tree	Fruit juice; D
Gloriosa spp.	Climbing lily	All parts
Hedera helix	English ivy	Leaves and berries
Helenium spp.	Sneezeweed	Whole plant
Helleborus niger	Christmas rose	Rootstocks and leaves; D
Heracleum lanatum	Cow parsnip	Leaves and root slightly poisonous; dangerous to cattle
Heteromeles arbutifolia	Toyon, Christmas berry	Leaves
Hyacinthus	Hyacinth	Bulb causes nausea, vomiting; may be fatal
Hydrangea macrophylla	Hydrangea	Leaves
Hymenocallis americana	Spider lily	Bulbs
Hypericum perforatum	St.-John's-wort	All parts when eaten; D

SCIENTIFIC NAME	COMMON NAME	POISONOUS PART OF PLANT
Ilex aquifolium	English holly	Berries
Impatiens spp.	Impatiens	Young stems and leaves
Iris spp.	Iris	Rhizomes; D; if eaten causes digestive upset but not usually serious
Jasminum	Jessamine	Berries fatal
Juglans spp.	Walnut	Green hull juice; D
Kalmia latifolia	Mountain laurel	Leaves
Laburnum vulgare	Golden chain	Leaves and seeds cause severe poisoning; may be fatal
Lantana spp.	Lantana	Foliage and green berries may be fatal
Laurus	Laurel	All parts fatal
Ligustrum spp.	Privet	Leaves and berries
Linum usitatissimum	Flax	Whole plant, especially immature seedpods
Lobelia spp.	Lobelia	Leaves, stems, and fruit; D
Lupinus spp.	Lupine	Leaves, pods, and especially seeds
Lycium halimifolium	Matrimony vine	Leaves and young shoots
Macadamia ternifolia	Queensland nut	Young leaves
Maclura pomifera	Osage orange	Milky sap; D
Malus	Apple	Seeds contain cyanic acid
Melia azedarach	Chinaberry	Fruit, flowers, and bark
Menispermum	Moonseed	Berries (resemble small wild grapes) may be fatal if eaten
Myoporum laetum	Ngaio	Leaves very poisonous
Narcissus spp.	Narcissus, daffodil	Bulbs cause nausea, vomiting; may be fatal
Nepeta hederacea	Ground ivy	Leaves and stems
Nerium oleander	Oleander	All parts extremely poisonous, affect the heart
Nicotiana spp.	Tobacco	Foliage

SCIENTIFIC NAME	COMMON NAME	POISONOUS PART OF PLANT
Ornithogalum umbellatum	Star-of-Bethlehem	All parts cause vomiting and nervous excitement
Oxalis cernua	Bermuda buttercup	Leaves
Papaver somniferum	Opium poppy	Unripe seedpod very poisonous
Pastinaca sativa	Parsnip	Hairs on leaves and stems; D
Philodendron spp.	Philodendron	Stems and leaves
Phoradendron spp.	Common mistletoe	Berries fatal
Pittosporum spp.	Pittosporum	Leaves, stem, and fruit very poisonous
Podophyllum	Mayapple	Apple, foliage, and roots contain at least 16 active toxic principals, primarily in the roots; children often eat the apple with no ill effects, but several may cause diarrhea
Primula spp.	Primrose	Leaves and stems; D
Prunus spp.	Cherry, peach, plum	Seeds and leaves; seeds contain cyanic acid
Quercus	Oak	Foliage and acorns; takes a large amount to poison

Mistletoe usually won't be touched by animals, but it is poisonous. However, birds eat the berries without harm.

Scientific Name	Common Name	Poisonous Part of Plant
Ranunculus spp.	Buttercup	Leaves; D; if eaten, irritant juices may severely injure the digestive system
Rhamnus spp.	Coffeeberry, buckthorn	Sap and fruit; D
Rheum rhaponticum	Rhubarb	Leaves; D; large amounts of raw or cooked leaves (contain oxalic acid) can cause convulsions, coma, followed by death
Rhododendron spp.	Rhododendron, azalea	Leaves and all parts may be fatal
Rhus diversiloba	Poison oak	Leaves; D
Rhus radicans	Poison ivy	Leaves; D
Ricinus communis	Castor bean	Seeds fatal
Robina pseudo-acacia	Black locust	Young shoots, bark, and seeds
Rumex acetosa	Sour dock	Leaves
Sambucus canadensis	Elderberry	Shoots, leaves, and bark; children have been poisoned by using the pithy stems for blowguns

All parts of the lovely rhododendron are very toxic if eaten.

Scientific Name	Common Name	Poisonous Part of Plant
Saponaria vaccaria	Cow cockle	Seeds
Sativus	Autumn crocus	Bulb; causes vomiting and nervous excitement
Senecio mikanoides	German ivy	Leaves and stems
Solanum dulcamara	European bitter-sweet	Leaves and berries
Solanum nigrum	Garden huckle-berry nightshade	Unripe berries and leaves
Solanum nudiflorum	Black nightshade	Green berries poisonous but apparently harmless when fully ripe
Solanum pseudo-capsicum	Jerusalem cherry	Fruit
Solanum tuberosum	Irish potato	Green skin on tubers
Tanacetum vulgare	Common tansy	Leaves
Taxus baccata	Yew	Foliage, bark, and seeds fatal; foliage more toxic than berries
Thevetia peruviana	Yellow oleander	All parts
Urtica spp.	Nettles	Leaves; D
Veronica virginica	Culver's root	Roots
Wisteria	Wisteria	Mild to severe digestive upset; children sometimes poisoned by this plant
Zephyranthes spp.	Zephyr lily	Leaves and bulbs

D = those plants likely to cause dermatitis (susceptibility varies from person to person)

Garden Plans

This chapter contains an assortment of garden plans to suit the different needs of different gardeners.

A Model Companion Garden

Planning your first organic garden may be a little tricky, but in time and with experience truly good gardeners get to know plants' likes and dislikes (which may sometimes vary in different localities), and they can spot just the place in their garden for any plant where it will do best.

Where it is at all possible, try to use double-purpose plants — those that are both decorative and sources of food, or those that are protective of other plants — in your garden.

Planning your garden on paper is one of the best ways to achieve success. Use large sheets ruled off into squares, using a scale of 2 feet to the inch. Draw large plants the size they will be at maturity. Locate existing features, such as trees, shrubs, hedges, buildings, and paths. This is important, as they may shade the garden during certain hours of the day. Mark off north and south on your plan. Then add each item you want in your garden, considering them in their order of importance to you and your family and the space and time you can give to them.

For your vegetable garden, plan on using and replacing early vegetables with those that do well in spring and summer. In turn these will be replaced with cool-season vegetables for the fall.

Keep records, for you will probably want to change your plan from season to season, including some new vegetables or different varieties and discarding others that may not have done well. Note how well certain plants did on certain sites, the effect of their form and color, and the rotation of your crops. Rotation is very important in garden plots that are planted year after year.

The heavy feeders (those that need generous fertilizing, including corn, tomatoes, cabbage, and other brassicas) should be followed by legumes to help the soil recover from the demands of the heavy feeders, especially in poorer soils. In a live humus soil legumes may go in third place if desired. The last group are the light feeders, which include root vegetables, bulbs, herbs, and protective flowers such as marigolds and nasturtiums.

For the serious gardener a complete record of space used and treated in a vegetable garden is an invaluable aid in planning the next year's garden. It is not enough to place the high vegetables to the north, the corn in blocks, and the asparagus where the tractor will not run it down. A map showing the pH factor in various garden areas should be made and kept up-to-date. Application dates of slowly available materials, such as rock phosphates, should be recorded. With such, you can make a long-range plan of your garden that will serve you well in future years.

Few garden projects are more fun to experiment with than companion planting. Good plant neighbors are those that occupy different soil levels, like beets and kohlrabi, or that find in each other's company the light requirements that best suit them. An example of this is the compatibility of celery and leek: The upright leek finds room near the bushy celery plant. Other compatible combinations are cabbage and beans, beets and onions, cucumbers and sweet corn, carrots and peas, cucumbers and beans, early potatoes and corn, early potatoes and horseradish, tomatoes and parsley. Asparagus beetles are repelled by tomatoes growing nearby. To repel the cabbage maggot, plant mint, tomato, rosemary, or sage in the next row. Radish will grow extra well and especially tender near lettuce.

A Model Companion Garden

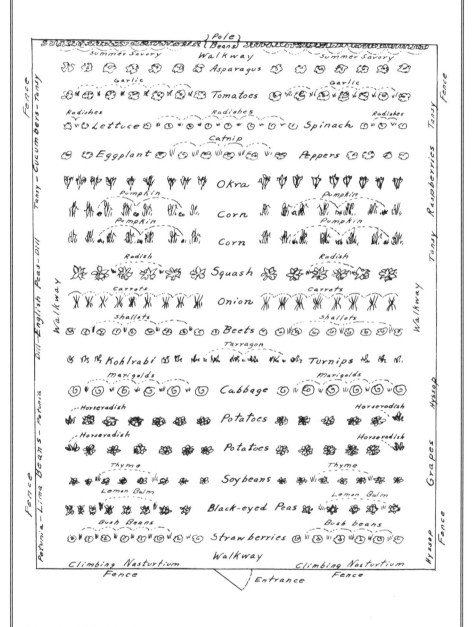

On the other hand, avoid the incompatible combinations such as sunflowers and potatoes, tomatoes and fennel, tomatoes and kohlrabi, pole beans and beets, pole beans and kohlrabi. Note, however, that localities and seasons also seem to affect "companions." More than one gardener has gleefully told me she planted onions with peas or beans and had a wonderful crop of both.

We are sometimes surprised when we go out into our garden in the morning to find that the bugs have held a candlelight ceremony and arrived overnight. Timing can discourage these unwelcome guests. I find fall-planted squash is entirely free of squash bugs. Onions around spring-planted squash help to keep insects away. Aromatic herbs as border plants are very helpful to the garden.

In the drawing opposite you see a model companion garden very much like my own (though smaller). Walkways around the fence inside make it easy to use a tiller. Note, too, how a protective fence is used for such climbing plants as beans, cucumbers, peas, and grapes.

Flowers add beauty to the garden but are chosen as well for their beneficial influences on crop vegetables and fruits. Note vegetable interplantings, too, in most of the rows. Perennials such as asparagus and horseradish are placed at the outsides to make tilling of the full garden easier.

The Weekend Garden

The primary object of the weekend garden is to get the "mostes' result with the leastes' effort." Remember that garden space may also be saved by doubling rows of narrow-growing crops. Thus, onions, which take only as much space as the diameter of the bulb, may be grown in double rows 6 inches apart. Mulch may be arranged between the two rows, when the plants are large enough, to cut down the amount of hand-weeding, if necessary. Carrots, beets, parsnips, and turnips may be handled in the same way. Cos or Romaine lettuce, which grows elegantly tall, is also a space saver and may be grown close together. Bush varieties of squash and cucumbers and beans also take less space.

Annual vegetables that like sole possession of their garden space for the entire summer include lima beans, Swiss chard, cucumbers, eggplant, okra, onions, parsley, parsnips, peppers, sweet potatoes, late white potatoes, salsify, squash — both summer and winter — New Zealand spinach (grows well in hot weather), and tomatoes.

Just because you are a weekend gardener doesn't mean that you cannot enjoy some of the perennial vegetables as well, if you are willing to plan for them and give them their own space. Asparagus, chives, horseradish, perennial onions, rhubarb, perennial herbs, and berries are possible, and most of these can stand a certain amount of benign neglect. They must, of course, be located where power tillage or cultivating tools will not be inconvenienced by them. Usually it's best to give them a plot of their own, removed from the rest of the garden.

Study your garden catalogs for small, space-saving varieties, even dwarf vegetables, as well as for early, midseason, and late varieties. If you have a gardening friend or neighbor, consult him as to the best varieties for growing in your area. Don't be shy — gardeners just love to give advice!

If your schedule allows you to garden only one or two days per week, here are some tips.

- Plan a small garden the first year.
- Prepare your garden soil in the previous fall, incorporating compost.
- Grow the vegetables your family likes best — choosing varieties that produce well in your area.
- Interplant some companion plants in each row.
- Plan for a watering system with a timer for use when rainfall is insufficient. Use a soaker hose in the garden.
- Harvest often to keep plants producing (peas, beans, tomatoes, peppers, okra, for example).
- Pull spent plants and replace with warm-weather plants either started indoors or purchased.
- As the season advances, start a fall garden in the shade of corn-stalks, etc., and pull when young plants are well started.
- Mulch plants to cut down on weeding. Plow in mulch in the late fall as preparation for early-spring planting.

The Weekend Garden

COOL-SEASON VEGETABLES

	COMPANION PLANT	HINDERED BY
BEETS	LETTUCE, ONIONS, CABBAGE	POLE BEANS
BROCCOLI	BEETS, POTATOES, ONIONS, CELERY	STRAWBERRIES, TOMATOES
CABBAGE	ONIONS, POTATOES, CELERY	" "
CARROTS	peas, lettuce, chives, radishes, leeks, onions	DILL
CAULIFLOWER	potatoes, onions, celery	STRAWBERRIES, TOMATOES
CHARD	LETTUCE, ONIONS, CABBAGE	POLE BEANS
KALE (OVERWINTERS)	LATE CABBAGE, POTATOES	WILD MUSTARD
LETTUCE	RADISHES, STRAWBERRIES, CUCUMBERS	
ONIONS	SUMMER SAVORY, camomile	peas and beans
ORIENTAL GREENS	STRAWBERRIES	
PEAS	CARROTS, TURNIPS, RADISHES, CUCUMBERS, AROMATIC HERBS	
RADISH	REDROOT PIGWEED, NASTURTIUMS, MUSTARDS	all cole plants
SPINACH	STRAWBERRIES	
TURNIPS	PEAS, hairy vetch	hedge mustard, knotweed

WARM-SEASON VEGETABLES

	COMPANION PLANT	HINDERED BY
BEANS, BUSH	cucumbers, strawberries, plant with corn	ONIONS
CHILI PEPPERS		
CORN	potatoes, peas, beans, cucumbers, pumpkin	TOMATOES
EGGPLANT	Redroot pigweed, green beans	
MELONS	MORNING GLORY	potatoes
OKRA	Bell peppers, eggplant	
SQUASH	icicle radishes, nasturtiums	
SWEET PEPPER	basil, okra	
TOMATILLO	basil	
TOMATO	chives, onion, parsley, basil, marigold, carrot. Do not plant next to corn.	

The Weekend Garden

COOL-SEASON VEGETABLES

PLANT	COMPANION PLANTS	HINDERED BY
Beets	Lettuce, onions, cabbage	Pole beans
Broccoli	Beets, potatoes, onions, celery	Strawberries, tomatoes
Cabbage	Onions, potatoes, celery, mint	Strawberries, tomatoes
Carrots	Peas, lettuce, chives, radishes, leeks, onions	Dill
Cauliflower	Potatoes, onions, celery	Strawberries, tomatoes
Chard	Lettuce, onions, cabbage	Pole beans
Chinese cabbage	Bush beans, marigolds, onions, sage	Pole beans, corn, strawberries, tomatoes
Kale (overwinters)	Late cabbage, potatoes, sage, marigolds, nasturtiums	Wild mustard
Kohlrabi	Beets, cucumbers, onions, sage	Pole beans, strawberries
Leeks	Carrots, celery, onions	Bush beans, pole beans, peas, soybeans
Lettuce	Radishes, strawberries, cucumbers	Pole beans, strawberries, tomatoes
Onions	Summer savory, camomile	Peas and beans
Oriental greens	Strawberries	
Parsley	Tomatoes	
Peas	Carrots, turnips, radishes, cucumbers, aromatic herbs	
Radish	Redroot pigweed, nasturtiums, mustards	All cole plants
Spinach	Strawberries	
Turnips	Peas, hairy vetch	Hedge mustard

WARM-SEASON VEGETABLES

PLANT	COMPANION PLANTS	HINDERED BY
Beans, bush	Cucumbers, strawberries, plant with corn	Onions
Chile peppers		
Corn	Potatoes, peas, beans, cucumbers, pumpkins	Tomatoes
Cucumber	Bush beans, pole beans, nasturtiums, corn, leeks, onions, peas, radishes, sunflowers	Potatoes
Eggplant	Redroot pigweed, green beans	
Melons	Morning glory	Potatoes
Okra	Bell peppers, eggplant	
Potatoes (early or late)	Bush beans, cabbage, corn, eggplant, marigolds, nasturtiums	Cucumbers, pumpkin, squash, sunflowers, tomatoes
Squash	Icicle radishes, nasturtiums	
Sweet pepper	Basil, okra	
Tomatillo	Basil	
Tomatoes	Asparagus, carrots, celery, chives, garlic, onions, parsley	Corn, potatoes

PERENNIAL VEGETABLES

PLANT	COMPANION PLANTS	HINDERED BY
Asparagus	Basil, parsley, tomatoes	—
Chives	Carrots	Bush beans, potatoes, peas, soybeans
Horseradish	Protective to potatoes	—
Perennial onions or shallots	Radish	—
Rhubarb	Seldom troubled by insects or disease	Cut off flowering growth as it takes nourishment from plant and reduces vigor

The Postage Stamp Garden

Whether the postage stamp garden is tucked away in the corner of a city backyard or blossoms in the rarefied atmosphere of a penthouse far above the traffic of the streets, it can bring the same rewards and satisfaction to its creator as a larger one of more impressive proportions. The small backyard garden on the ground may be cared for much the same as a larger garden would be and with good soil, water, and sufficient sunlight may be expected to have much the same degree of success.

But city gardening in high places is different from that in a city backyard. High above the street, dust and fumes may not be troublesome but there are other problems to deal with — excessive winds and beating sun. A certain amount of experimentation as to the placement of the garden will best determine the location most likely to be successful.

Because the roots of the plants are confined to limited quarters in their box or boxes, the soil must be prepared with care. It should be composed of sandy loam (topsoil), humus, and peat moss. Fertilizers such as decomposed manure and bonemeal should be mixed in the soil. Good drainage is essential.

Plants can be protected from high winds by windbreaks of various kinds, such as a fence of cedar saplings, a perpendicular board fence, or one of close basketweave. For a more decorative effect, use a screen of plate glass, glass brick, or other interesting material.

Plant as many started plants as possible, such as tomatoes, peppers (sweet and hot), onions, and herbs. Okra transplants well, so you might try growing a number of plants in a pot, setting them in when they are larger where you want them to grow. Yellow squash and zucchini can be grown in peat pots and handled the same way. All of these plants do well in sunshine if given wind protection. Avoid lettuce and other shade-loving plants. But you might like to tuck in here and there a few sun-loving flowers such as marigolds and nasturtiums, which can also do double duty as protection from insects. Yes, you may be surprised at the number and variety that will find their way to your garden! Some, serving as pollinators, are not all bad.

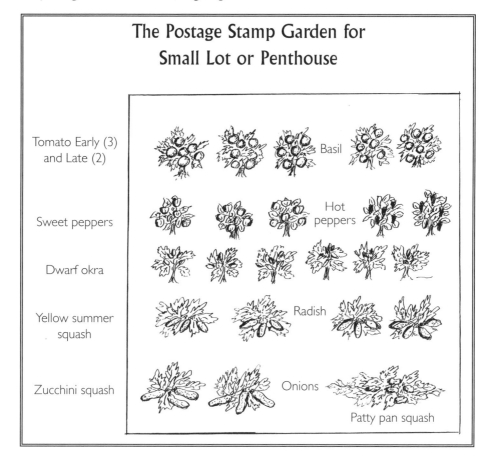

The Postage Stamp Garden for Small Lot or Penthouse

Tomato Early (3) and Late (2)

Basil

Sweet peppers

Hot peppers

Dwarf okra

Yellow summer squash

Radish

Zucchini squash

Onions

Patty pan squash

A roof garden may not be as easy as one on the ground but can be a lot of fun to plan, plant, and care for. To the confirmed gardener, having this miniature plot means not just having fresh vegetables for your table but also the joy and satisfaction of "growing your own." For the city dweller a "garden in the sky" may be just the stuff that dreams are made of.

Tips for Roof Gardening

Soil. Use a good, friable loam. Fertilize with dried manure. Be sure the roof is strong enough to support a box or boxes. It's advisable to check with a structural engineer.

Mulch. A mulch will help prevent sudden drying out of the soil from wind and sun. Use peat moss, decomposed manure, leafmold, or black plastic.

Vegetables. With full sun, good soil, and boxes about 8 inches deep, you can grow broccoli, parsley, radishes, bush beans, endive, onions (from sets), New Zealand spinach, Swiss chard, small-size tomatoes, and short-rooted carrots and beets. Cage peppers, standard-size tomatoes, and bush squash for wind protection.

Herbs. Herbs are a good choice for shallow boxes usually used on a roof. Try thyme, chives, parsley, mint, sage, and basil.

Flowers. Marigolds, zinnias, ageratum, petunias, calendulas, sweet alyssum, lobelia, portulaca, celosia, iberis, forget-me-not, salvia, coreopsis, aster, and scabiosa are all good choices. Many now come in dwarf varieties.

Boxes. Boxes should be deep enough to hold 8 to 12 inches of soil. Make them as wide as you wish or your space will accommodate. Provide drainage holes in the bottom of each box. Paint the insides with asphaltum, or other wood-preserving compound, and the outside with several coats of quality outdoor paint. Dark green is a good color. Cypress or redwood has good durability.

Vines. Vines are possible if the wind is not too strong. An arbor over part of the roof would make a good vine support and also supply some shade and shelter. Try ivy, honeysuckle, or morning glories.

The Kitchen Herb Garden

Why have a culinary herb garden adjacent to your kitchen door? For the simple reason of convenience and quick accessibility. Whether you are a busy houseperson or a busy businessperson, you want to give your family the most inviting and taste-tempting meals you can prepare in the shortest possible time. Those of us who cook with herbs and delight in their flavor, fragrance, and freshness find this small kitchen garden a little luxury that is pleasurable, affordable, and easily obtainable, well worth the small amount of time its maintenance requires.

Most herbs originated in rather dry, often rocky soil and do best in soil that is lightly fertilized. Most herbs like sunlight, though some will do equally well in shade. And fresh herbs add that certain something hard to achieve with dried.

Basil. You haven't really lived until you have tasted fresh basil with tomatoes. This sweet, wondrous-smelling plant is at its very best when used fresh. Pesto is that delicious Italian sauce made with fresh basil pounded with olive oil, pine nuts, parmesan cheese, parsley, garlic, salt, and pepper. Use it on spaghetti or green noodles, spread on toasted bread, or on vegetables and in salads.

Fresh bay leaves make up the ubiquitous bouquet garni that is used in many meat and vegetable dishes, noodle dishes, condiments and soups.

Thyme. Jeanne Rose, in *Herbal Guide to Food*, describes the thyme as a little plant with a big flavor. It is available in an incredible range of scents and flavors from nutmeg, caraway, mint, pine, and pepper to lemon, citronella, and many more. Thyme is delicious in stuffings and salads, on vegetables such as beans, onions, and tomatoes, and in herb butter and breads. Try out several varieties and surprise family or guests with unusual flavors.

Mint in its variations can liven up many things besides that time-honored southern favorite, mint julep, usually flavored with spearmint or peppermint. White mint is especially useful in jellies or with lamb. Apple mint can be used to scent and flavor salads. Pineapple mint, ginger mint, and peppermint can be used in teas.

Mints are good in breads and stuffings, with vegetables, in soups, or with eggs, meats, or game. Many sauces can be given a delightfully tangy flavor with the use of various mints.

Marjoram is indispensable in French cooking. It is used as a garnish, in soups, salads, eggs, cheese, vegetables, meat or poultry, stuffings, pasta, breads, and drinks.

Parsley. I need not dwell on the uses of parsley as it is so well known and universally used, so pretty and reliable in the herb garden. Just remember that it is an extremely rich source of minerals and vitamins as well, including vitamins A and C.

Chervil is another herb essential to French cooking, and one that we need to show more respect. Try seasoning peeled avocados with olive oil, pepper, lemon juice, and a really generous dose of chopped chervil. Or use it generously sprinkled over cold cream soups, fresh green salads, carrots, or potatoes.

French tarragon. You can achieve herb happiness in your culinary art with French tarragon, often called the king of culinary herbs. Its tart, somewhat sweet licorice taste adds excitement to béarnaise or hollandaise sauce. Jeanne Rose suggests basting a roasting chicken with tarragon-mushroom butter. (See Suggested Reading.)

Sage, an old kitchen favorite, is used to counteract the greasiness of fatty meats. It is used in stuffings of goose, duck, turkey, and chicken, and it is also good with rabbit, eggs, cheeses, beans, onions, and tomatoes.

Summer savory is good chopped into salads or with baked fish or roasted pork.

Rosemary is one of the most important herbs. Even the flowers are put into salads, and the herb is used for everything from garnishes to desserts and jellies.

To those accustomed to using only dried herbs, the truly fresh ones from your own kitchen garden will open up a whole new world of epicurean excitement.

A Kitchen Herb Garden

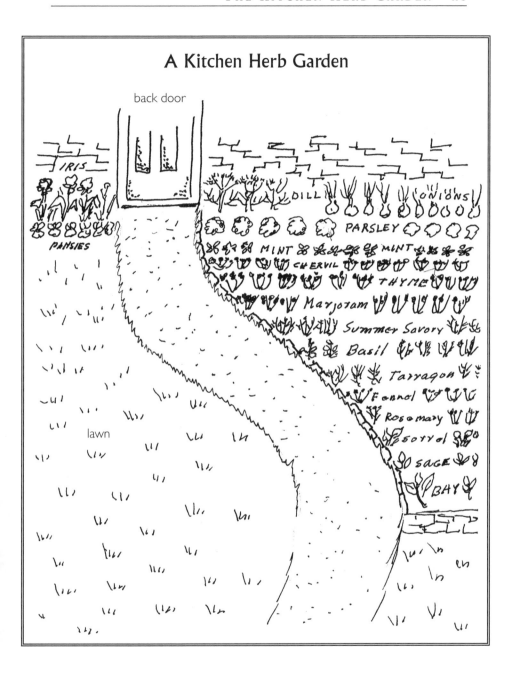

back door

IRIS

PANSIES

DILL

ONIONS

PARSLEY

MINT   MINT

CHERVIL

THYME

Marjoram

Summer Savory

Basil

Tarragon

Fennel

Rosemary

Sorrel

SAGE

BAY

lawn

A Child's Garden

A little yard where children can play and have their own garden should be located where soil, sun, and drainage conditions are good — preferably in the service area where it can be watched from the house.

Water should be available nearby. Part of the playhouse may be used as a storage area.

Plant trees and shrubs that do not bear unwanted fruit for children to nibble on, fall on, or track into the house.

Plant a grass that can "take it," such as bluegrass, fescue, or Bermuda.

Use concrete or asphalt to build a "drag strip" for riding toys — making wide places for "turn-out stations."

Use chain-link fence or a similar type with clear visibility.

Floodlights, mounted on adjacent buildings or in trees or on a high pole, can add hours of evening playtime.

Buy started plants for the kids' garden, varieties that are quick and easy to grow, or prolific producers such as squash. If the child is old enough to help tend the garden, be lavish with praise when something of his or hers is brought to the table.

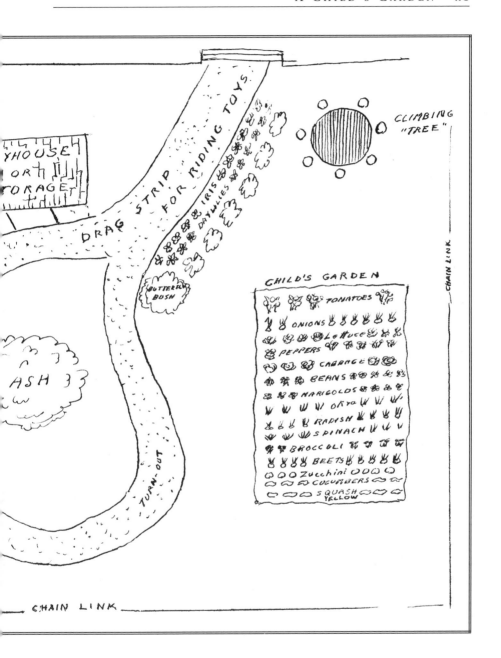

The Able Disabled Gardener's Garden

A "no-stoop garden" is the nicest kind! Here are some suggestions to make a convenient garden for an older or disabled person.

- Box (or boxes) should be of a height easily reached by the individual.
- Boxes can be any length but should be just wide enough to be easily reached from either side.
- Box should be sturdy enough to support gardener, if using cane, walker, or wheelchair — also sturdy enough for soil when wet.
- Elevating an area improves drainage. Holes should be bored in the bottom of the box and in the pan underneath the box.
- Use a watering can with a comfortable handle and detachable sprinkler head. Try using a spray wand.
- For a larger garden you may want an overhead spray arrangement. For spot watering, use ice cubes; they'll melt slowly with little drip. Set a plant or two beneath the drip.
- Cover holes with copper screening to prevent plugging up.
- What will you grow? Just about anything you want to. Have planter boxes of different depths.
- Harvest often and keep a "floating crop game" going, quickly reseeding harvested plants.

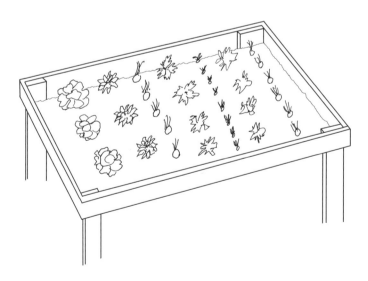

Choose your tools carefully and buy good quality. You will not need a garden tractor but at the very least you should have a digging tool, a clipping tool, and a cultivator tool. Kathleen Yeomans, writing in *The Able Gardener,* suggests that you "test-drive" before you buy. "Lift them," she says, "and manipulate the tool from the position in which you will be using it. Whether you stand, stoop, or sit to garden will determine the handle length you require. If you expect to be sitting while you garden, sit down and go through the motions of using the tool." Buy tools that fit your hand comfortably, especially if you have unusually small or extra-large hands. A tool that seems heavy in the store will feel twice as heavy when you are working with it in your garden.

Your little garden can be caught in a late freeze just like a big one. Have some type of hot cap handy to protect tender plants. In a pinch use grocery bags, weighted down with stones or clods. Remove them during the day if the weather is warm.

Keep a sharp eye out for insects that may suddenly discover your garden, often overnight, if they are in the immediate neighborhood. Seeing them almost eye to eye in the elevated garden makes them easy to spot and you can quickly take care of the problem. Just be sure they are "enemies" and not beneficial kinds.

Give careful thought to the location of your elevated garden. Will it receive full sunlight for at least six hours of the day? Will a large tree shade it morning or afternoon? Does it have protection from the wind? And is it located convenient to your degree of disability, if you garden from a wheelchair, standing with a cane, or using a walker?

And I urge you most sincerely not to let yourself get too tired. This is supposed to be fun, but sometimes we get carried away and just want to keep going. Take it from me, for I, too, am an "able disabled" gardener with weak hands, small strength, and painful arthritis.

VEGETABLE GROWING GUIDE FOR MINIGARDENS

Group 1: Plant seeds of these vegetables in large containers (bushel baskets or 5-gallon buckets). They need full sunlight and warm weather. These vegetables should be planted outdoors when it is warm and the danger of frost is past. You can start tomato and pepper plants indoors six to ten weeks early, then move them outdoors at the proper time for earlier harvest.

VEGETABLE	DAYS TO HARVEST	PLANTING DEPTH	PLANTS PER CONTAINER
Tomato	140–150	$1/2$"	1
Green pepper	140–180	$1/2$"	1
Hot pepper	140–180	$1/2$"	1
Bush squash	50–60	$3/4$"	1
Eggplant (use hybrid miniature)	50–60	$1/2$"	1

Group 2: These vegetables can be grown in pots 6 to 10 inches. They can withstand a little shade and do well in cool weather. Plantings should be made when it is warm and all danger of frost is past.

VEGETABLE	DAYS TO HARVEST	PLANTING DEPTH	PLANTS PER CONTAINER
Mustard greens	30–60	$1/4$"	4
Leaf lettuce	45–60	$1/4$"	4–6
Turnips	55–65	$1/4$"	3–4
Green onions	90	$1/4$"	2–3
Chives	80	$1/4$"	2–3
Radishes	25	$1/2$"	2
Beets	60–80	$1/2$"	2–3
Parsley	65–75	$1/4$"	1

Don't plant onion seed. Use dry sets or green plants, or use an onion from the kitchen that has sprouted; usually it will divide itself into several plants.

The Tinest Garden of All

Life can be very lonely for the elderly, housebound, or disabled. But how they can enjoy butterflies! Julia Percival and Pixie Burger give us a suggestion in their book *Household Ecology*. "Often you can persuade butterflies to settle and feed on a sunny windowsill if offered the right confection. This confection is simple. Half a teaspoon of honey and half a teaspoon of sugar mixed in a cup of warm water will make an adequate butterfly nectar.

"To make a feeder use a saucer and a wad of cotton. Butterflies taste through their feet, so they need an island of cotton in the middle of the nectar sea. The cotton will absorb the honey-water so that the butterfly, when it lands on the cotton, will taste the food through its feet and then it will stand on the island and lower its rolled tongue and suck the nectar up."

The Spirit Garden

When our ancestors first happened on the formulas for making wine and beer, it was considered a tremendous boon from the gods. Alcohol was supposed to have an in-dwelling spirit adopted from the life of the fruit and plants from which it was made. Hence the origin of our modern term "spirits" for such drinks.

Beers, wines, brandies, cordials, bitters, and whiskeys can all be made from the herbs, fruits, grains, vegetables, and trees in your garden. (See the plan on pages 202–203.)

The Spirit Garden

Trees

Persimmon, wine
Sassafras, root beer
Peach, wine, brandy; washed
  peelings plus a few stones
  can be used to make brandy
Pear, wine
Fir; Native Americans used
  the young treetops to make
  a beer said to prevent
  scurvy
Plum, wine
Lime, wine additive
Lemon, wine additive
Orange, wine
Apple, wine, cider
Cherry, wine, cordial
Elderberry, wine
Birch, beer

Vines

Hop vine, beer
Honeysuckle, wine
Grape, wine

Vegetables (fully mature)

Parsnips
Potatoes
Beets
Carrots
Turnips
Rhubarb
Pumpkin
Hard-shelled winter squash

Herbs

Anise, used to flavor liqueurs
Wintergreen, wine
Ground ivy, bitters
Sage, wine
Maguey (Agave species),
  tequila
Nettle, beer

Flowers

Daisy, flower heads, wine
Dandelion, flower heads, wine
Roses, petals
Clover, flower heads, wine

Berries

Blackberry, wine, cordial
Raspberry, wine
Cranberry, wine
Strawberry, wine
Boysenberry, wine
Dewberry, wine
Various hybrids

Weeds

Barberry, wine
Burdock, beer, bitters
Red currant, wine
Black currant, wine
Gooseberry, wine
Wild grape, wine
Wild hops, beer, ale
Juniper, beer
Red mulberry, wine

Wild sarsaparilla, wine
Shadbush (Juneberry, service-
    berry), wine
Wild strawberry, wine

Beverage Additives

Lemon, sangria blanca
Lime, margarita
Orange, tequila sunrise
Pineapple, piña colada
Tomato, sangria
Jalapeño chile, sangria
Onion, sangria
Coconut milk, piña colada
Mint — sprigs to mint julep

Whiskey

Corn, chief ingredient of
    Bourbon whiskey
Rye whiskey, rye is chief
    ingredient
Barley malt, Irish whiskey
Barley malt, Scotch whiskey

The Spirit Garden

SASSAFRAS

BIRCH

PERSIMMON   PEACH

PEAR

HOP VINE   ELDER
4NISE   BERRY   GRAPE
                          VARIETIES

BLACKBERRY   RASPBERRY   CRANBERRY

DAISY   DANDELION   ROSES

NETTLE   SAGE

COCONUT   MILK OOO JALAPENO chili PEPP

PARSNIPS   POTATOES   BEETS

VARIOUS GRAINS   PUMPKI

Barberry   Burdock Red & Bla

wild Grape   Wild Hops, Juni

Shadbush   ooo

Rye ....

LIME

LEMON

PLUM   APPLE   ORANGE

CHERRY

FENCE

HONEYSUCKLE

CORN   MAGUEY

ERGREEN

ERRY   BOYSENBERRY   DEWBERRY   PINEAPPLE

LOVER   GROUND IVY

X   WINTERGREEN

ONIONS   TOMATOES

ARROTS   TURNIPS   RHUBARB

HARD RIND WINTER
SQUASH
rrant Gooseberry

Red Mulberry, Wild Sarsaparilla

Strawberry

arley

The Aphrodisiac Herbal Window Box

Hundreds of effective aphrodisiacs have been discovered over the centuries. Many can achieve amazing results. Virility can be sustained, preserved, and even recaptured with specially selected herbs and foods.

Many herbs have proved effective as aphrodisiacs through the ages. They include basil, chervil, chives, mint, parsley, sage, tarragon, thyme, and garlic.

Soup, meat, fish, and desserts featuring the aphrodisiacs grown in your own garden can become powerful sexual stimulants. Suburbanites, with a small plot of land behind their house, can supply themselves with aphrodisiacs in abundance, but what of apartment dwellers who have no scope whatever for ordinary gardening? Must they be penalized because they have chosen (or been forced by circumstances) to occupy part of a building that is surrounded, not with the good earth, but with concrete, asphalt, or paving stones? Are they to be deprived of the pleasure and satisfaction of growing their own "contributory crops"?

Fortunately, the answer to these questions is "No," an emphatic "No!" Experiments have shown that a great deal can be achieved in that very small garden — the window box. While such small-scale gardeners cannot expect to produce the same quantity and variety as the owner of 600 square yards, neither do they need to. They can provide themselves with a surprisingly large number of herbs and vegetables of a stimulating nature, quite often sufficient to their needs.

Assuming that the apartment has a living room, bedroom, and kitchen, and that each has an average-sized window, each window box can accommodate a reasonable selection of plants. In fact, even one window box can grow a succession of herbal or vegetable plants, if you change them from time to time.

Chives can be grown from seeds. The chopped leaves give a distinctive flavor to salads and a pleasing, tangy taste to soups and egg dishes. A bit milder than onions, they improve chicken and shrimp dishes. Chicken broth with chives, yolk of eggs, and powdered almonds makes an invigorating nightcap.

Garlic as an aphrodisiac is second to none. The trouble with garlic is its powerful odor. If a garlic-flavored dish is prepared, it should be shared.

Mint, on the other hand, has a delightful fragrance. It is a powerful amatory aid and can be said to stimulate the appetite. A meal of lamb, new potatoes, and peas can be deliciously enlivened with a mint sauce, doing something more than satisfying hunger. Even boiled cabbage sprinkled with this herb may leave one in "mint" condition.

Parsley. The aphrodisiac properties of parsley were appreciated by the ancient Greeks and Romans. Parsley is just chock-full of vitamin E. Parsley is more than just a pretty face; use it lavishly as a stimulating addition to boiled chicken and omelettes.

Thyme. That oldest and most attractive of kitchen herbs, thyme, can be grown either from seed or by root division. As an aphrodisiac it crops up with almost monotonous regularity in world literature. Far, far back in time it was found invigorating by the Egyptians. John Gerard in his *Herball,* written in 1633, praises it; and Benedictine monks still use it as an ingredient in their liqueurs. Use discreetly, for a little goes a long way, and it tends to kill other and more subtle flavors.

Vegetables. While some apartment dwellers may choose to concentrate on herbs and fill their window boxes with only basil, tarragon, fennel, rosemary, lavender, and so on, others might prefer to add a few stimulating vegetables such as radishes, dwarf carrots, spinach, peas, and beans, all of which have been shown to be "contributory crops."

Cress. Another possibility is cress, the aphrodisiac properties of which have been recognized for thousands of years.

Oysters. If you like raw oysters, fine; if not, try them in a creamy stew with parsley, celery, and mushrooms.

Plan 1

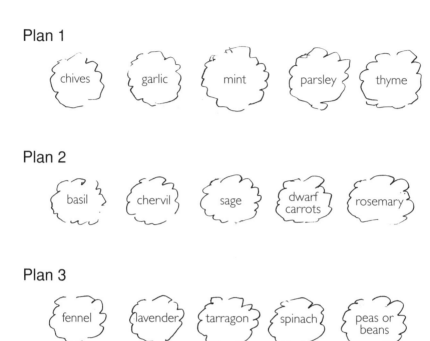

chives   garlic   mint   parsley   thyme

Plan 2

basil   chervil   sage   dwarf carrots   rosemary

Plan 3

fennel   lavender   tarragon   spinach   peas or beans

Three garden plans for window boxes

Construction of Box

Measure window ledge. Box should be a few inches shorter in length than the window ledge of the same width and no more than 6 inches high. Use well-seasoned lumber, oak if possible. Spray interior with paraffin and apply match. Let surface oil burn off and then extinguish flame by turning box upside down. Paint outside of box. Color should harmonize with surroundings. Bore half-inch hole at five or six intervals in bottom of box for drainage and aeration. Nail small wedges of wood on base of box to keep box level and clear of the sill. Wedges should be high enough so shallow tray may be pushed under box to catch surplus water. In ends of box, screw metal hooks that will fit into wall staples and hold box securely in position.

In bottom of box put a layer of broken crocks or oyster shells to cover drainage holes. Second layer should consist of dead leaves, decayed turfs, and straw. Over this put good loam, filling box to within an inch of top. A bushel of soil is usually ample.

Invest in a small-spouted can for watering. Foil placed behind box will reflect sunlight most herbs need.

Sources

Businesses relocate frequently. We try, but it is not always possible to keep our lists up-to-date. See your local extension agent for additional sources.

Bio-Dynamic Farming and Gardening Association
262-649-9212
www.biodynamics.com
Books, DVDs

Burgess Seed & Plant Co.
309-662-7761
www.eburgess.com
General nursery plants

Farmer Seed and Nursery
507-334-1623
www.farmerseed.com
General nursery plants

Henry Field's Seed and Nursery Co.
513-354-1495
http://henryfields.com
General nursery plants

Gurney's Seed & Nursery Co.
513-354-1492
http://gurneys.com
General nursery plants

Nichols Garden Nursery
800-422-3985
www.nicholsgardennursery.com
Rare herbs, vegetable seeds

Park Seed Co.
800-845-3369
www.parkseed.com
Herb, vegetable seeds

Richters Herbs
800-668-4372
www.richters.com
Seeds and plants

Spring Hill Nurseries
513-354-1510
http://springhillnursery.com
General nursery plants

Stark Brothers Nurseries & Orchards Co.
800-325-4180
www.starkbros.com
Fruit and nut trees

Stokes Seeds
800-396-9238
www.stokeseeds.com
Untreated seeds

Van Ness Water Gardens American Water Gardens, Inc.
800-205-2425
www.vnwg.com
Water lilies

Suggested Reading

Some of these books may be out of print but can be found at your local library, or purchased secondhand.

Ajilvsgi, Geyata. *Butterfly Gardening for the South*. Dallas, TX: Taylor Publishing, 1991.

Campbell, Stu. *Mulch It!*. North Adams, MA: Storey Publishing, 2000.

Creasy, Rosalind. *The Complete Book of Edible Landscaping*. San Francisco, CA: Sierra Club Books, 1982.

Gibbons, Euell. *Stalking the Wild Asparagus*. Chambersburg, PA: Alan C. Hood & Company, 1988.

—————. *Stalking the Healthful Herbs*. Chambersburg, PA: Alan C. Hood & Company, 1989.

Philbrick, Helen, and Richard Gregg. *Companion Plants and How to Use Them*. Old Greenwich, CT: Devin-Adair Pub., 1990.

Riotte, Louise. *Catfish Ponds and Lily Pads*. North Adams, MA: Storey Publishing, 1997.

—————. *Roses Love Garlic*. North Adams, MA: Storey Publishing, 1998.

Rodale's All-New Encyclopedia of Organic Gardening. Emmaus, PA: Rodale Books, Inc., 1993.

Rose, Jeanne. *Herbs & Things, Jeanne Rose's Herbal*. New York: Berkley Publishing Group, 1972.

Telesco, Patricia. *A Kitchen Witch's Cookbook*. St. Paul, MN: Llewellyn, 1994.

Telesco, Patricia. *Folkways*. St. Paul, MN: Llewellyn Publications, 1995.

Index

Page references in *italics* indicate illustrations; **bold** indicates charts.

Grow Your Gardening Knowledge with More Books from Storey

Epic Tomatoes by Craig LeHoullier
Grow your best tomatoes ever with this fascinating and artful guide that's packed with everything tomato enthusiasts need to know about raising more than 200 hybrid and heirloom varieties.

Gardening with Less Water by David A. Bainbridge
Tackle any drought with these inexpensive, low-tech methods for using water more efficiently in your garden. Illustrated, step-by-step instructions teach you to deliver water directly to roots, reduce weed growth, harvest rainwater, and much more.

High-Yield Vegetable Gardening
by Colin McCrate & Brad Halm
Bring your home garden to its fullest potential with practical advice and handy tables to guide you through preparing the soil, selecting crops, mapping out a garden plan, managing pests, and more.

The Vegetable Gardener's Bible, 2nd Edition
by Edward C. Smith
This best-selling vegetable gardening classic features a proven system for growing an abundance of organic vegetables, fruits, and herbs in your own backyard using wide rows, raised beds, and deep soil.

Week-by-Week Vegetable Gardener's Handbook
by Ron Kujawski & Jennifer Kujawski
These detailed, customizable to-do lists break gardening into manageable tasks. Whether you're planting strawberries, pinching off pumpkin blossoms, or checking for tomato hornworms, this invaluable resource shows exactly what to do — and when and how to do it.

Join the conversation. Share your experience with this book, learn more about Storey Publishing's authors, and read original essays and book excerpts at storey.com. Look for our books wherever quality books are sold or call 800-441-5700.